ETHICAL OCCURRENCES IN GOVERNMENT CONTRACTING:
PRINCIPLED OR CORRUPT?

Sandra G. Haynes

BALBOA.
PRESS
A DIVISION OF HAY HOUSE

Balboa Press books may be ordered through booksellers or by contacting:

Balboa Press
A Division of Hay House
1663 Liberty Drive
Bloomington, IN 47403
www.balboapress.com
1 (877) 407-4847

Because of the dynamic nature of the Internet, any web addresses or links contained in this book may have changed since publication and may no longer be valid. The views expressed in this work are solely those of the author and do not necessarily reflect the views of the publisher, and the publisher hereby disclaims any responsibility for them.

The author of this book does not dispense medical advice or prescribe the use of any technique as a form of treatment for physical, emotional, or medical problems without the advice of a physician, either directly or indirectly. The intent of the author is only to offer information of a general nature to help you in your quest for emotional and spiritual well-being. In the event you use any of the information in this book for yourself, which is your constitutional right, the author and the publisher assume no responsibility for your actions.

Any people depicted in stock imagery provided by Thinkstock are models, and such images are being used for illustrative purposes only.
Certain stock imagery © Thinkstock.

Print information available on the last page.

ISBN: 978-1-5043-4379-4 (sc)
ISBN: 978-1-5043-4410-4 (hc)
ISBN: 978-1-5043-4409-8 (e)

Library of Congress Control Number: 2015918589

Balboa Press rev. date: 11/12/2015

CONTENTS

ABSTRACT

The Office of the Inspector General in the Department of Justice reported cases of government contracting employees accepting bribes totaling over $540 million within a 6-year period. Framed by the stakeholder theory, this qualitative case study included government contracting individuals from the mid-Atlantic region as purposefully sampled participants who answered 8 open-ended questions concerning government contracting managers' understanding of the knowledge required to diminish unethical behaviors of government contracting employees who administer contracts. Member checking strengthened credibility and trustworthiness of the interpretation of participant responses. Data from semistructured interviews and company documents were analyzed, coded, and then grouped into categories using a modified content analysis technique. Key themes suggested that to mitigate government contracting employees' unethical behaviors, government contracting managers require continued training, trust is vital to disseminating ethical requirements to employees, and there are benefits to conducting ethical government contracting. Findings and recommendations from this study may contribute to positive social change by improving training and ethical standards in government contracting, which could lead to enhancing societal trust in government contracting organizations.

Key words: Acquisition, Ethics, Trust, Government Contracting.

DEDICATION

To know what you know and what you do not know, that
is true knowledge.

-Confucius

First, foremost, and always, my thanks to GOD for giving me the strength,
courage, and determination to make it through this challenging journey.
Second, I dedicate the pursuit of this degree (and the many long hours
and sleepless nights) to my daughter Phelicia (You are Extraordinary.
From your positive outlook to your total honesty; I can always count on
you to give me that extra push I need), my son Eriq (You are exceptionally
brilliant. You see the world through lenses that I wish others could see. You
always rise above and make me want to do more), and my mother Mrs.
Mahala Haynes (You inspire me to reach for the clouds). To all my family
and friends who have encouraged and supported me in this journey, thank
you. I appreciate and value your love, faith, compassion, and support. I
could not have accomplished such a monumental task by myself. Thank
you for being my strength. Love…..Always.

PREFACE

The liabilities of government contracting employees' unethical behaviors persist and cause mistrust by society. The promise of ethical government contracting is in jeopardy. The issue of government contracting employees' unethical behaviors occurs globally and across all spectrums and all organizations. Examples of unethical behaviors in government contracting include employees taking bribes worth more than $500 million dollars. At this point, it is not so much that we are surprised at the presence of corruption in government contracting, but it seems that there is still not enough focus on the problem and what it takes to prevent the corruption.

This publication is designed to be a summary of the requirements government contracting managers need to assist their employees in mitigating unethical behaviors when doing government contracting business. The focus is on a few individuals in one government contracting organization. No claim to original government contracting works or representation of any government contracting organizations.

The publication is based on interviews with a small group of subject matter experts. Every effort has been made to present individual's views clearly and concisely. Reasonable efforts have been made to publish reliable data and information, but the author and publisher cannot assume responsibility for the validity of all materials or the consequences for their use.

Every effort has been made to minimize the use of acronyms. Commonly used acronyms are spelled out the first time that they are used. References correspond to *superscript* numbers listed at the end of sentences.

ABOUT THE AUTHOR

Sandra G. Haynes claim a long history of involvement with government contracting as a U.S. Navy Storekeeper, U.S. Government Contracting Officer, and U.S. Government Contracting Manager. Haynes is a Doctor of Business Administration who dreams of one day seeing government contracting free of the negative stigma with regards to ethics.

Haynes addresses ethics in government contracting by highlighting elements of the contracting process and presents views from government contracting subject matter experts regarding requirements needed to mitigate government contracting employees' unethical behaviors. The areas covered include the basics of government contracting, process and issues, ethics, social objectives of government contracting, authority, and stakeholder role in government contracting.

Haynes also enhances the academic literature on ethics in government contracting; this publication can be used in courses that teach ethics and government contracting. This is a work that is needed in the discussion of government contracting ethics. It serves to move the subject of ethics in government contracting to the forefront where it belongs.

FORWARD

Money is the driving force for everyone; those who provide a service and those who receive this service. This creates immense problems when it comes to dealing with each other. Some want more for personal reason and others want more just to upgrade their lifestyle. Of course there is nothing wrong with wanting more money; it is a vital part of a free and not so free enterprise system. The challenge with money is the way in which we go about procuring it.

The quest for more money does lead to questions of ethics in the civilian world and more so in the public sector where these individuals are responsible for the public purse. While I may not be seen to have been an expert in this field, the arguments presented by Sandra Haynes in this book is stirring and interesting. She tackled the complicated world of integrity amongst government employees with relation to exploring the causes and possible resolution to the issue.

Sonia Nadina Haynes - Author

1

THE BASICS

A single, uniform source of standards of ethical conduct and ethics guidance shall be maintained within the Department of Defense (DoD), and each DoD Agency shall implement and administer a comprehensive ethics program to ensure compliance with such standards and guidance (DoD 5500.07-R).

1.1 Introduction to Ethics in Government Contracting

Personal conflict of interest among government contracting personnel is an important area in government contracting in which clear, concise, and up-to-date regulatory coverage is urgently needed. The Federal Acquisition Regulation (FAR) lists statutory regulations to guide employees who perform acquisition support functions under contracts awarded by federal government organizations. In 2009, new developments were implemented in an attempt to curtail the rise of corruption and unethical occurrences in government contracting.

To act ethically or unethically is the question that employees face when administering government contracts. According to the Office of Personnel Management (OPM), government contracting employees may solicit, evaluate, negotiate, and award contracts to any contractor, vendor, or supplier authorized to do business with government contracting organizations. These employees should uphold the highest standards of ethical integrity since their job requires exercising judgment over public funds.

Federal government contracting is an important component in the United States' success. These organizations are major participants in the acquisition of goods and services from public and private entities, and Congress has enacted statutes and regulations that guide government contracting policies and values. Recent increases in government spending have contributed to unethical behaviors by government contracting employees.[157] To combat this, the Department of Justice (DOJ) has allocated financial resources to fight against contracting fraud. The Office of the Inspector General (OIG), overseen by the Inspector General, monitors and tracks the use of taxpayer dollars through assessments, evaluations, examinations, and inquiries. The Inspector General is required to keep Congress updated about any concerns noted regarding the use of taxpayer funds.

With unethical behaviors continuing to plague the government contracting arena, researchers struggle to fine reasons for such occurrences. Unfortunately, no consensus exists, either about why unethical behaviors occur or about how to prevent them. Contributing to the problem, vaguely defined regulations do not provide enough transparency in the contracting process;[31] furthermore, government contracting organizations may not be clearly defining ethical standards.[125]

In the past decade, unethical behaviors by some government contracting employees have increased.[36] Since 2005, increases in unethical behavior by government employees have been reported by the Government Accountability Office (GAO); however, there was a reduction in employees who revealed knowledge of unethical behaviors. For example, employees have taken unauthorized gifts in exchange for unwarranted contracts.

It is highly unethical and improper for government contracting employees to work outside the confines of the FAR (Federal Acquisition Regulations) requirements. As unethical behaviors by employees continue, researchers attempt to understand what leads to such behaviors. This trend in abuse of ethics generated an impression of widespread ethical violations in government contracting organizations.[36] In addition, workplace culture might influence unethical behavior.[122]

1.2 Who Is the Government Contracting Employee?

Although government contracting employees have been subject to an extensive set of personal conflict of interest rules under statute and Office of Government Ethics (OGE) regulations, unethical behaviors by those individuals still plague government contracting organizations. Is it necessary to be ethical in government contracting? Is it acceptable for government contracting employees to take gifts from contractors doing business with the government? Are government contracting employees mindful of ethics in their business relationships with contractors? Government contracting employees are faced with challenges of ensuring that their decisions are ethical and comply with precise standards of conduct whenever doing government business.

In light of recent scandals involving government contracting personnel, we can note that government contracting ethics are not what they used to be. In recent years, business between employees and contractors became a teaming approach. The days of the government conducting business at arms' length are gone. Due to teaming with contractors, one might argue that the government has relaxed its ethical standards in government contracting. Is teaming between government contracting and contractors beneficial to the government or does teaming present employees with ethical challenges and obstacles? Some people postulate that these changes have improved business relationships between government contracting organizations and contractors. Still others speculate that the government has opened avenues for their employees to be unethical. Regulators' mandate is to prevent fraud, waste, abuse, and corruption government contracting; however, government contracting is still plagued with scandals and controversies.

What is ethics? *Merriam Webster* defines *ethics* as a set of principles that governs the individual. However, before we can determine what ethical standards an employee is required to follow, we should first understand who the government contracting employee is. The Office of Personnel

Management (OPM) classifies the contracting employee series (1102) this way:

> Positions in the contracting series are concerned with:
> (1) soliciting, evaluating, negotiating, and awarding contracts with commercial organizations, educational institutions, nonprofit organizations, and State, local or foreign governments for furnishing products, services, construction or research and development to the Federal Government; (2) administering contracts by assuring compliance with the terms and conditions of contracts, including resolution of problems concerning the obligations of the parties; (3) terminating contracts by analyzing, negotiating, and settling claims and proposals; (4) analyzing and evaluating cost or price proposals and accounting systems data; (5) planning, establishing, or reviewing contracts, programs, policies, or procedures; (6) formulating and administering policies and procedures to insure achievement of Federal socioeconomic goals, such as those affecting small business, labor surplus areas, and disadvantaged business firms; (7) developing acquisition strategies and directing or managing procurements; and (8) providing staff advisory services in one or more of the specializations in this occupation (OPM, 1983, retrieved from http://www.opm.gov).

As we can see, government contracting employees wear various hats. Can we then say these individuals are experts in their fields? Are they qualified, extensively trained individuals who are versed in the fundamentals of government contracting? We would hope so. The aforementioned employees are known by different names. Some may say they are civil servants, some may call them GS employees, and still some may simply call them thieves. Yes, *thieves*.

You may be scratching your head on the last description. Why would anyone describe these experts as thieves? Well, this is where our dilemma begins.

The United States Office of Government Ethics has a division dedicated to preventing conflicts of interest within the executive branch of the government. With so many agencies under one umbrella, there became a need to establish one uniform regulation to govern all employees of the Executive Branch. On February 3, 1993, 5 C.F.R. Part 2635 was codified and directed so that the aforementioned employees were now regulated by a set standard of ethical conduct for employees of the executive branch.

Managers and supervisors are required to emphasize ethics and moral integrity during annual ethics training. Federal government contracting employees must avoid negative behaviors such as bribery, misappropriation of public funds, fraud, conflicts of interest, payoffs, and kickbacks when doing their jobs. The public is watching. What a few employees do may have negative and lasting effects on what is thought about the entire organization.

We see it every day. How many times have we picked up a newspaper, turned on the television, gotten a news ping on our smartphones, or read an article on the Internet regarding another government employee scandal? Have you asked yourself why? What is causing the negative behavior? What can be done about it? In addition, **when will it stop?**

To answer those questions, I decided to take a journey to a group of subject matter experts (SMEs). Not experts in the area of bribery, fraud, and kickbacks, but experts in the area of contracting. Those individuals may have witnessed the above behaviors or may have insights into the cause and effect of the whys of said behaviors. Let us start with the experts. We do not need to go back very far to find cases of employees taking bribes from contractors. For example, in July of 2010, the Department of Defense (DoD) Standards of Conduct Office, a part of the Office of General Counsel published cases concerning U.S. federal government contracting employees convicted of unethical conduct. Cases included employees who used their positions to award unapproved contracts. One employee received fifteen years in prison for accepting bribes to issue contracts to unqualified organizations, while another who accepted bribes was fined more than $250,000 in addition to a prison sentence.

Authority

5 C.F.R. (Code of Federal Regulations) Part 2635
DoD (Department of Defense) 5500.07-R
Federal Acquisition Regulation (FAR)
Office of Personnel Management (OPM)

Note: "Always do right; this will gratify some people, and astonish the rest." (M. Twain)

1.3 The Problem

This behavior is detrimental to government contracting organizations because it threatens the national defense and increases wasteful spending of taxpayer funds. When employees fail to act ethically, the reputation of the previously mentioned organizations deteriorates. In 2013, the Department of Justice Office of the Inspector General reported cases of employees accepting bribes totaling more than $540 million within a six-year period.[134]

The general business problem of this study, as mentioned previously, the Inspector General noted increases in occurrences of unethical conduct, but the number of employees willing to reveal such occurrences has decreased. In addition, oversight by government contracting managers has not alleviated such unethical behaviors. One might argue that managers lack the knowledge required to regulate unethical behaviors.

1.4 The Case

The purpose of this qualitative case study was to provide an understanding of the knowledge required by managers to regulate unethical behaviors of government contracting employees. This study formed the basis for researching and understanding the worth of management and leadership development in government contracting.

What is value-based performance? The concept of value-based performance is grounded on a customer-oriented system centered on ethical values. Incorporating principles of competence raises an organization's ethical performance standards. For an organization to demonstrate value, it must incorporate core principles into its performance base. In value-based management within an organization, managers must ensure they consistently maximize ethical principles and pass them on to their employees.

Government contracting personnel from an organization in the mid-Atlantic region participated in semi-structured interviews to share their insights about the strategies needed to limit employees' unethical behaviors. The completion of this study will help managers learn strategies to reduce unethical behaviors within their organizations. Findings from this study may also contribute to positive social change by improving training and ethical standards, which could enhance society's trust in government contracting organizations. In addition, the study might encourage socially accountable, transparent federal contracting processes that reduce fraud.

Questions for Review:

How is ethics defined? (*Remember: there is no one right answer.*)

Who is the deciding factor on what is or is not ethical?

Why would a government contracting employee behave unethically when administering government contracts?

What may cause the negative behavior?

What can be done about it?

1.5 Nature of the Study

The inquiry used for this study is a qualitative case analysis. Qualitative researchers collect, analyze, and interpret data based on participants' characterization of real-world events.[95] In contrast, quantitative researchers use statistical data and hypothesis to draw conclusions.[96] As a mixed method approach combines both qualitative and quantitative data to reach conclusions, such an approach will not be suitable for this study since it would require including statistical data from a quantitative study.[117] A primary aim of conducting this qualitative case study is to communicate an understanding of the individual's insights. Conducting this study allowed me to focus on a particular case, incorporate rich description of the circumstance, and provide heuristics by illuminating the reader's understanding of the phenomenon.[54]

A qualitative researcher classifies the study based on the research design. Strategic research for qualitative studies include case study, narrative study, ethnography, grounded theory, and phenomenology.[181] The research question determines the appropriate research design.[95]

A single case study design comprises the nature of this study. Although both single and multi-case studies involve interviews, data management, and interpretations, a multi-case design does not fit this study, because it involves researching a collection of embedded cases to find a suitable meaning.[173] The single case study method allows qualitative researchers to retain holistic and significant characteristics of events such as individual life cycles as well as organizational and managerial processes.[199] As a result, narrative, ethnographic, grounded theory, and phenomenological designs did not suit this study.

Narrative researchers seek to understand the life of an individual for the purpose of relaying stories about the experiences of that individual.[174] Using narrative research for this study was inappropriate because the focus for this study was on the understanding required by a group of mid-level managers in a specific organization. The unit of analysis in ethnography is the study of a culture-sharing group[151], which was not the goal for this study. In grounded theory, the qualitative researcher attempts to develop a theory based on data from participants in the field.[66] Since grounded theory may be inductive in nature because it involves building a theory from the *bottom up*[81], it was not suited for this study. With a phenomenological study, the goal is to describe and show the merging and differing interrelations of a phenomenon on participants in the research.[53] The goal for this study was not to study several individuals commonly engaged in their experiences. Neither was there a plan to describe participants' personal experiences. The case study design provided a means for me to focus on a single entity.

A concise question was central to the research process. Arriving at a topic and question that had social significance was challenging. There is no guide to creating a research question, and each research question results in a different outcome.[57] Likewise, creating quality research questions assists researchers in gaining and maintaining the interest of individuals.[192] Therefore, to understand the knowledge required by individuals managing government contracting employees, I created this research study to answer one precise question: What knowledge do government contracting managers need, in order to mitigate unethical behavior of government contracting employees when administering contracts?

Questions for Review:

What issues might government contracting managers have in encouraging employees to behave unethically?

What fundamentals might a manager use to assist government contracting employees in understanding how to perform their duties ethically?

What are the elements of the organization's philosophy that a manager might use to address government contracting employees' unethical behaviors?

What challenges might a manager confront in determining ethical implementation of the organization's philosophy?

What training and/or development methods can managers use to guide employees to act ethically?

How can training and/or development methods be improved and incorporated as an integral part of government contract administration?

What benefits can be derived from employees' ethically administering government contracts?

1.6 Conceptual Framework

Stakeholder theory, advanced by Freeman, formed the conceptual basis for this study. The concept of stakeholder theory should encourage business managers to consider the principles of organizational and public ethics when determining business compliance.[71] Freeman devised concepts that integrated ethical notions into corporate strategies.[55] The conceptual framework of this study incorporated a review of participants' views regarding strategies that government contract managers need to reduce employees' unethical behaviors. The conceptual framework of this study aligned stakeholder values with the idea of ethical/unethical behaviors by employees when administering government contracts.

The literature review contains a discussion of stakeholder theory addressing three concepts: shareholders' value and its association with business success, threats to stakeholder values, and strategies for bridging the gap between organizational values and employees' ethical principles. These principles may assure business success, moral integrity, corporate ethics, and positive social change. The stakeholder theory and the link to ethics and integrity affect (a) individuals' right to liberty, opportunity, and freedom, and (b) stakeholders' influence on governing principles that correlate with ethics. Considering the organization and people over self is altruistic. Government contracting employees should consider their actions and their impact on society and the public trust. Organizational leaders cite the need for public trust in promoting organizational values and codes of ethics.[145] Government contracting organizations can use stakeholder theory to administer government contracts.

1.7 Assumptions, Limitations, and Delimitations

Qualitative research comprises a variety of techniques, ideas, methods, themes, limitations, and assumptions.[87] A qualitative researcher should be aware or his or her assumptions in order to reduce bias.[74] This section lists the assumptions, limitations, and delimitations of this study.

1.7.1 Assumptions

This study contained four assumptions. The first assumption was that deficiencies existed regarding government contracting employees administering government contracts at the chosen establishment. The second assumption was that the culture of the organization provided employees unlimited access to government contracting suppliers. Due to the nature of the participants' jobs, employees might make unauthorized contact with some suppliers. Another assumption was that government contracting organizations lacked ethical training. The last assumption was that leadership felt detached; therefore, they did not understand why unethical occurrences took place.

1.7.2 Limitations

The limitations of this study may prevent presenting clear, unbiased analysis; therefore, contemplating these limits benefited the presentation of the findings of the study. The first limitation was that focus on a single case study of one organization might limit generalization of the study over other government contracting organizations. The second limitation was regarding participants' knowledge of government contracting. Although participants were in Pay Grades GS-11 to GS-13, there was no way to determine how acquainted they were with the subject matter. The Office of Personnel Management (OPM) required participants to receive specific training; however, each person's view of the information may have been different. The final limitation regarded concern for a lack of individuals willing to participate in this study.

1.7.3 Delimitations

An optimal sampling would consist of employees from all government contracting organizations. Government contracting employees in Pay Grades GS-11 to GS-13 working at one organization in the mid-Atlantic area comprised this study. This delimitation was necessary, as the focus of this study was in determining management knowledge needed to reduce contracting employee unethical behaviors. For applied reasons, interviewing the entire government contracting population fell outside the scope of this study. Twenty individuals represented an appropriate sample size in this qualitative study. Although some universities that conduct research studies may require a minimum sample size, it is important to continue the interview process until data saturation is reached. Twenty-one individuals participated in this study.

1.8 Significance of the Study

As mentioned before, the intent of this study was to consider participants' insights regarding management knowledge needed to reduce unethical behaviors by government contracting employees. One earlier researcher focused on increased government spending as the precipitator of employees' unethical behaviors.[157] Yet another researcher concentrated on ethical principles and the impact of employees' unethical conducts.[36] Each researcher focused on different causes for the unethical behaviors; however, the results of employees' unethical conducts are interconnected.

2

BUSINESS ETHICS AND GOVERNMENT CONTRACTING

In 1989, the President's Commission on Federal Ethics Law Reform recommended that individual agency standards of conduct be replaced with a single regulation applicable to all employees of the executive branch. Acting upon that recommendation, President Bush signed Executive Order 12674 on April 12, 1989. That Executive Order was modified under Executive Order 12731 and set out fourteen basic principles of ethical conduct for executive branch personnel and directed OGE to establish a single, comprehensive, and clear set of executive branch standards of ethical conduct. OGE published the Standards of Ethical Conduct for Employees of the Executive Branch on August 7, 1992. The regulation became effective on February 3, 1993, and was codified in 5 C.F.R. part 2635.

2.1 Introduction – Business Ethics Influencing Government Contracting?

In qualitative research, a literature review provides the basis for research and gives conditions for the development of the research question. A researcher creates new knowledge from the literature review. The main resources for the literature review incorporated journals and peer-reviewed articles. The following databases provided content for the literature review: Sage Premier, Business Source Complete, ScienceDirect, Academic Search Complete, and Thoreau. Content searches consisted of keywords (*acquisition, competence, conflicts of interest, contracting, corporate governance, ethics, government contracting, outsourcing, procurement, qualitative research, and trust*) as noted in the definition of terms. Results of the searches yielded more than 400 articles for review. The amounts of articles to cogitate were significant; however, the only articles incorporated enhanced the literature review. The focus of the articles covered business ethics, government contracting, and government contracting compliance and regulations.

2.1.1 Contribution to Business Practice

The result of this qualitative, case study might help the government contracting managers in developing strategies to reduce employees' unethical behaviors. As previously stated, an essential problem is an increase in unethical behaviors by employees when administering government contracts. Additionally, there was a noted decrease in employees willing to disclose such unethical behaviors.

2.1.2 Implications for Social Change

The results of this research study may have a positive effect on the issue of ethics when administering government contracts; and provide a standard for government contracting managers to determine ethical guidelines, procedures, and training for government contracting employees. Positive social change in government contracting is possible. Change becomes possible when society, policy makers, acquisitions, and contracting workforces understand transparency in the government contracting process.[172] This study may contribute to social change by producing ideas that could reverse financial losses that occur through government contracting employees' unethical behaviors. Government contracting managers' understanding of how to reduce employees' unethical behave may diminish future occurrences. Benefits of this study may encourage socially accountable and transparent federal contracting processes that might reduce fraud. Findings and recommendations from this study may contribute to positive social change by improving training and ethical standards, which could lead to enhancing society's trust in government contracting organizations.

Authority

5 CFR 2635-Standards of Conduct for Employees of the Executive Branch

10 US Code § 2304

10. U.S.C. § 2307

41 U.S.C. 423 - Procurement Integrity Act

48 C.F.R. § 37.104(b)

American Recovery and Reinvestment Act

American Society for Public Administration

Armed Services Procurement Act of 1947

Competition in Contracting Act

Defense Acquisition Regulations Supplement

Executive Order 12674

Executive Order 12731

Federal Acquisition Streamlining Act

Federal Acquisition Reform Act of 1996

Federal Property and Administrative Services Act of 1949

Procurement Integrity Act (41 U.S.C. §423)

Title 48 of the U.S. code of regulations

Title VII of the Civil Rights Act of 1964

Under Article I, Section 8, Clause 18

2.2 Reflecting on Business Ethics in Relation to Government Contracting

Unethical occurrences may adversely affect public administration organizations.[13] When determining the most ethical contracting decision when administering government contracts, employees may encounter duplicitous problems. Making the best assessment may be a matter of personal choice or a business decision.[14] If there are legal or regulatory statutes involved, the decision is not always clear. When a government contracting employee makes an ethical decision contrary to government contracting guidelines, the employee may receive punitive action.

Business ethics has been pushed to the forefront of organizational strategy and corporate governance.[68] The study of business ethics seeks to understand why individuals in organizations conduct themselves in certain manners.[79] Ethical compliance is a prerequisite to good business ethics.[127] Society must be able to depend on the ethical standards of an organization; the organization should stress employee compliance with the rules, regulations, and integrity as set forth by organizational ethical standards and behaviors.

The moral burden of negotiating pressures between normal expectations and personal beliefs is daunting.[34] As such, employees' ethical decisions when administering government contracts may involve conflicting issues of determining what is morally right. When considering business ethics, organizations should ensure that ethical judgments constitute a regard for history.[61] Historical, ethical business decisions (i.e. *moral decisions* - the decision not to take a bribe, or *decisions having to do with ethics* - decisions about what business people are allowed to do) have changed the dynamics and structure of organizational morals and values.[56] Although employees may encounter occasions in which unethical behavior would be to their advantage, following government contracting guidelines may assist them in making ethical decisions.

Nothing in government contracting business should be outside of ethics; ethics must be the overruling consideration in every interaction between contracting employees and contractors. If government contracting organizations do not impose regulations and guidelines on their employees, employees will make ethical decisions based on personal judgment.[65] If government contracting organizations do not impose regulations and guidelines on their employees, employees will make ethical decisions based on personal judgment. It's plain that personal judgment is not always reliable; the default mode for some people is unethical behavior.

Individuals have unique values that guide them; however, when doing contracting business, the stated government ethics should guide the individual. Let's take for example Darleen Druyun, former Deputy Undersecretary of the Airforce. Druyun inflated prices on contracts to Boeing with whom she had accepted future employment. One could argue that unfortunately, this individual was not guided by ethical principles; she was guided by immoral values.

Government contracting employees may believe that if they are not caught, they are not guilty of unethical actions. If government contracting employees continue to behave dishonestly, they worsen society's attitude towards government contracting organizations.

The government procurement system underwent a major overhaul in the late 1980s. In 1988, Operation Ill-wind detailed extensive unethical exchanges between government contracting employees and suppliers.[33] Operation Ill-wind was a three-year operation, generated by the

Federal Bureau of Investigations (FBI), that looked at corruption with government contracting workers and defense contractors. Because of the investigation, at least sixty individuals were convicted of various unethical behaviors, including bribery, accepting illegal gratuities, and defrauding the government. Based on the scandal produced by Operation Ill-wind, Congress passed the 1988 Procurement Integrity Act. The Procurement Integrity Act (41 U.S.C. §423) as outlined in FAR 3.104, prohibits employees from knowingly obtaining contractor bids or proposals from defense contractor except as provided by law. If a government contracting employee serves in a position of authority with regard to a contract valued at $10 million or more, that employee cannot accept employment from the contractor receiving the award within one year of awarding the aforementioned contract.

Although Congress has enacted additional regulations to prevent unethical exchanges, government contracting employees continue to behave dishonestly. Ethics in government contracting can be as simple as doing what is right. It is not useful to society for any employee to give unfair advantage to a supplier/vendor when determining who receives government contracts. Government contracting is a strategic tool to bring diverse groups and cultures together, but ethics is essential to the development of government contracting.

Understanding the role of private companies in government contracting may be beneficial to understanding how ethics affects government contracting policy. During the past few decades, government contracting has become more prevalent.[80] Different sectors of society including the political arena have affected government contracting business. Persons who effect political change should understand how those changes affect individuals and society. Politicians/public managers have influenced government contracting policy.[19]

Unethical occurrences in large companies can present challenges when corporate leaders manipulate regulatory policies to ensure that cases of unethical behaviors dissipate.[186] Private companies may receive a government contract award simply because of their connections with a particular political party.[100]

A politicization of the government contracting process resulted in military wasteful spending while outsourcing contracts.[241] For example, representatives of the federal government coerced contractors to make purchases at inflated prices as conditions for continuing to received lucrative government contracts. In response to this coercion, in 1940 Congress amended the Hatch Act which prohibited political contributions from contractors. Attempts have been made by members of both political parties to amend the Hatch Act; however, to no avail.

In 2011, President Obama pondered issuing an executive order that required bidders on federal contracts to disclose all their political contributions to federal contenders and party committees. In addition to their own contributions, companies also would have had to disclose donations made by their officers and directors to political parties. As it stands, contractors and bidders are prohibited from making contributions to political parties; however, officers and directors of such organizations are not required to report their contributions. The proposed executive order was scrapped due to bipartisan opposition.

Government contracting organizations and employees may need further reforms; as such, the process of accountability while administering government contracts became stringent after 2008.[100] As assessed by Rousseau, individuals who affect political change should understand how those changes affect individuals and society.[184] Since government contracting organizations use private companies to do government business, ethical guidelines are necessary to clarify the interaction between government and the private sector.[27] The American public expects government contracts to be handed out, and completed, in an ethical and competent manner.

Because political influence can affect the execution of organizational regulations, organizations should move towards further oversight regarding political influence in government contracting.[25] If government contracting employees continue to act dishonestly when administering government contracts, the behaviors may continue to influence society's attitudes towards government contracting organizations. Acceptable oversight of government contracting transactions should hold the contractor accountable for ethically fulfilling terms of the government contract; inadequate oversight may lead to unfulfilled contract terms. Although politics may affect the administration of government contracts, positive ethical attitudes regarding government contracting might demonstration a balance between government contracting organizations' values and society's expectations.

In government contracting, both the government contracting employees and the suppliers have an obligation to conduct government contracting business ethically. Corporate executives, suppliers, and vendors, as well as government contracting employees, should exercise restraint and be morally responsible when doing government contracting business.[127] Government contracting requires transparency, equity, and ethics.[167] Government contracting organizations should work to improve their ethical climate.[199]

An organization's economic climate is dependent on current financial market trends.[76] Sudden changes in financial market conditions may produce financial crises. In 2008, the United States experienced one of the worst economic crises in recent history.[180] Although the 2008 financial crisis appeared minor on a global scale, the instability of the financial market affected most U.S. companies. The FAR outlined requirements regarding private entities desiring to do business with government contracting organizations. The words contractor, supplier, and vendor are interchangeable throughout this study.

The words *contractor, supplier,* and *vendor* are interchangeable throughout this study. As stated in FAR Part 9, subpart 9.1, an authorized contractor, vendor, or supplier should have sufficient financial resources to perform the tasks as required in government contracting. The contractor or supplier should have satisfactory performance record, a satisfactory record of integrity, and business ethics. All authorized suppliers/vendors should have equal opportunities to compete for government contracts.

Business ethics change based on society's perceptions of fairness, justice, and impartiality.[179] Stakeholders' trust in an organization is not automatic; the need to provide evidence of organizational ethics becomes apparent when stakeholders have input into the construct of organizational values.[8] Business ethical values are in constant transition. Society's views of organizations change more rapidly than changes can occur within the organization. Due to reports of extensive corporate scandals, society has lost faith in business integrity.[13] Society is skeptical of organizations and their employees doing business ethically.

As previously stated, perceived unethical behavior can diminish consumer/society's trust.[134] A strong reputation for ethical behavior by the organization and its members enhances consumer/society's trust. Business ethics is at the forefront of organizational strategy and corporate governance.[191] Strong business ethics produce positive corporate governance, to an organization's competitive advantage. Unethical factors can affect an employee whether doing business with a private company or government contracting entity. Knowing the organization's ethical requirements may help the employee when doing their job.

Business ethics arise from the needs of different stakeholders to provide standards by which to evaluate the ethicality of the organization.[193] The need to provide organizational ethics becomes apparent when stakeholders have input into the construction of organizational values.[147] To understand what general forces drive ethical or unethical conduct in business, organizations may analyze the effects of various individual events on ethical decisions.

Stakeholders who demonstrate too much faith in the organization become vulnerable. Vulnerability in business ethics affects stakeholders.[20] Stakeholders place trust in one person or group, therefore, leaving themselves vulnerable to ethical violations. Unethical behaviors in business can affect government contracting stakeholders.

2.3 Stakeholder Theory

The awareness of stakeholder theory dates back to 1963 and is based on Marxist-capitalist ideals.[45] It was not however until 1984 that Freeman introduced the concept of stakeholder management as an approach with regards to individuals and groups who affect the organization.[55] Freeman explained the need for strategically incorporating social concerns into day-to-day business decisions by including stakeholders in the decision-making process. The concept of stakeholder theory encourages organizational employees to combine principles of corporate and public ethics with corporate compliance.[171]

While stakeholder theory is crucial to understanding different aspects of organizations, limited knowledge exists regarding the value of stakeholder theory and its measurement.[69] In this study, stakeholder theory highlighted ethics, shareholders, and the relationship to government contracting. Stakeholders might preserve their interest by acting against an organization.[72] The atmosphere of government contracting is conducive to instances of unethical behaviors when administering contracts.[31] From 2000 through 2009, government contracting spending increased from $1,702 billion to $2,938 billion. Vague regulations reduced transparency in the government contracting process.

Organizations can deter fraud through personal and organizational regulations.[148] Government contracting organizations might discourage unethical behaviors through ensuring ethical compliance with government contracting regulations. Ethical compliance within government contracting should focus on the broader area of stakeholder management and social responsibility.[10] Government contracting employees may have their own agendas; however, compliance with government contracting policies may improve the employee's ethical performance.

Proponents of stakeholder theory associate corporate and social ethics with corporate ethical compliance.[144] Freeman's stakeholder theory allows formation of a philosophy to guide an organization's ethics and provides stakeholders with alternative viewpoints from which to explore the link between ethics and business.[88] Government contracting managers should consider the public trust in the company they are managing, and the impact that trust or lack of trust has on the company's stakeholders, including the larger society. Corporate social responsibility affects all stakeholders.[10] Corporate social responsibility incorporates ethics and morality within an organization. To maintain society's trust, organizations should develop standards that apply to all stakeholders.[163] Organizational ethics is a matter of compliance with applicable laws.[161]

Opponents of stakeholder theory assert that managers use the advantages of stakeholder theory to influence resources that benefit the organization.[51] Stakeholder theory is manipulative and deficient in ethical approaches to stakeholders and is therefore considered unimportant to the organization. Ethical obligations comprise an organization's social change. Society criticizes and abhors organizations that cannot demonstrate positive influences.

Stakeholder theory concepts are instrumental in providing managers and employees with new perspectives to explore the relationship between ethics and business.[88] Three concepts are considered in stakeholder theory. The first concept looks at a capitalist model which favors the success of shareholders.[171] Theorist favoring concept 1 overlooked the interest of other stakeholders and restricted some advantages that might progress from stakeholder theory. In Concept 2, theorists feared a focus on stakeholders would threaten the success of an organization.[171] Proponents of this idea assessed stakeholder identification might prove difficult to define, therefore creating a financial or business threat to the organization. Theorists recognize limits to potential benefits within this concept because of the level of importance placed on the stakeholder. A balanced approach to stakeholder theory embraces cooperation between the organization, stakeholders, and shareholders. Theorist favoring concept 3 supports the integration of ethics into corporate strategy. Theorists believe that organizations should embrace the interest of its shareholders and stakeholders.[23] Government regulation and corporate best practices should embraced the interest of its shareholders and stakeholders to reduce fraud.

Government contracting employees tasked with upholding the public interest should offer to society and all stakeholders both ethics and integrity. Stakeholder value should resonate throughout the organization. Businesses should create and illustrate moral values for their stakeholders. When discussing organizational strategies, government contracting organizations should consider stakeholders' interests. When applying stakeholder theory to organizational policies, all individuals and groups who may be affected by the activities of the company should be considered.[55]

Stakeholder theory consists of two sections: the ethical and managerial branches. Although both branches focus on preservation of the organization, the ethical branch considers all stakeholders while the managerial branch emphasizes power within the organization.[39] An organization's alignment and the stakeholders' strategies may affect society's trust. Organizational success should consist of the ethics and moral characteristics its stakeholders.[6] It is not enough to think internally; stakeholder strategists must think globally.

Companies should encourage their employees to fulfill their responsibilities to society.[129] Maintaining the stakeholder's and the public's trust is vital to an organization's success. Companies should deliberate the stakeholder's needs when considering organizational responsibilities.[195] Aligning accountability in contracting relationships might help in keeping the public trust.[193] Businesses should plan ethics and transparency guidelines to assist employees in enforcing business and community values when safeguarding the public trust.[89] Deontological ethics safeguard organizational veracity by cautioning individuals to avoid wrongdoings that violate the public trust.[1] Society looks to public sector employees to act ethically and trustworthy. Government contracting employees should strive to ensure compliance with organizational values and applicable laws. To have a clear understanding of what ensures fairness and impartiality when administering government contracts, organizations develop detailed requirements and guidelines to assist employees in doing their jobs.

2.4 Corporate Governance

The government contracting arena established principles to assist employees in fulfilling their duties for the benefit of the stakeholders. In response to the collapse of WORLDCOM, ENRON, and other large corporations, Congress enacted the Sarbanes-Oxley Act (SOX) of 2002. SOX protects stakeholders from fraudulent practices in the business industry.[76] Corporate governance emerged from the collaboration between investors, managers, and employees.[132] Collaboration ensured respect and appreciation of each stakeholder's contribution. In the focus on corporate governance, each member is responsible for ensuring that ethical standards are a focal point of the collaboration.[16]

A strategic foundation, embodying values, policies, and goals, is necessary to the success of any organization.[97] Ethical corporate governance reflects the company's efforts to address legitimate responsibilities, thereby building a foundation of ethical business practices.[63] Unfortunately, high-profile corporate scandals continue to reveal unethical corporate governance. Media reports have exposed wrongdoing in some government contracting organizations as well as in private business. Businesses exist to create corporate value, but some organizations may not care about the relationship between organizational and stakeholder values.[94] Sound corporate governance enhances the company's reputation.[78] Society observes the sustainability of an organization's corporate governance through the actions of stakeholders.[82] Corporate governance in government contracting depends on the balance of organizational principles, stakeholder's values, and government contracting employees' enforcement of the government contracting organization's ethical agenda.

Organizations must focus on ensuring that the company meets the expectations of the customers and supports the stakeholders' needs. Each venue requires ethical corporate governance.[156] Corporate governance and ethical values have significant effects on stakeholder and employees' perceptions of the organization.[159] Social and environmental responsibilities necessitate compliance with ethical corporate governance codes.[6]

To understand the impact that varying values have on corporate governance, it is important to look at the impact of organization structures, employees' principles, and society's expectations. Complementary views between stakeholders are useful to corporate governance.[7] For example, socially responsible companies are often most respected and show greater profits. Companies with a good corporate governance are also more respected and valued.

Government contracting employees follow rules and guidelines to ensure that organizations and employees maintain effective corporate governance.[1] Although political influences may affect organizational regulations, corporate governance factors may be difficult to assess since each company's variables are self-determined. Government contracting organizations use corporate governance to set the organization's objectives and specify the rules and regulations used to monitor the policies, actions, and decisions of the organizations.

2.5 Government Contracting

The government obtains goods and services through contracts with private businesses. An enhanced understanding of government contracting provides insight for this qualitative case study. For the government contracting process to function, someone must have the authority to acquire goods and services. Government contracting involves purchasing goods and services from sources outside of the company. Government procurement of goods and services benefits everyone without exception, meaning that each stakeholder benefits individually.

Government contracting organizations must be open to competition. The FAR contains guidelines for competition in government contracting. To execute a standard competition process, contracting employees must make public announcements giving suppliers the opportunity to compete for government contracts.[136] FAR part 15 establishes requirements for choosing suppliers. Selecting a reputable contractor is necessary for contract management success.[18] The contracting employees should consider a supplier's past performance and reputation to determine if the supplier's actions may adversely affect the outcome of the contract.

In 1994, Congress passed the Federal Acquisition Streamlining Act (FASA), authorizing government contracting organizations to consider a supplier's past performance when determining future contract actions. Ignorance concerning vendors' past performance had contributed to high risk in contracting.[18] Without adequate contractor past performance information, government contracting organizations risk duplicating contract failures. Although contracts must be competitive, government employees must take into account a contractor's past performance when awarding contracts. Within the confines of stringent contracting regulations, allowing for consideration of past performance gives a small space for common sense to work in. However, government contracting organizations should demonstrate consistency when assessing a supplier's eligibility for a government contract. Employees who know the requirements of government contract management may do their job effectively. Contract management promulgates relationships between each government contracting organization, employee, and supplier. Suppliers may help government contracting employees with processes of contract administration provided the actions do not alter or affect other suppliers. Government contracting organizations should develop an understanding of appropriate economic, social, democratic, and legal considerations as highlighted by organizational requirements and civil law.[196]

The use of private suppliers to execute government contracts has increased in the past decade.[157] Government contracting-out or outsourcing affords private sector companies opportunities to provide goods and services to government organizations. Government contracting organizations posit that outsourcing to private companies provides cost savings in the delivery of services.[90] The government contract is an agreement that stipulates business communications between qualified private companies and the government.

Some of these qualified companies are small businesses. Since its foundation in 1953, the Small Business Administration (SBA) has worked to help small companies in the United States. Small businesses are vital to the U.S. economy since they can provide stability in economically distressed areas.[162] Due to small businesses' value to the economy, the SBA initiated policies and programs to maximize small business development. Because of recent financial crises, the government established public policies to support small business concerns.[41] The creativity and innovation of small businesses led to economic recovery in the United States.

In 1953, Congress created the Small Business Administration (SBA), whose function was to assist, counsel, and protect, as much as possible, the interests of small business entities. The SBA was directed to ensure that small businesses received a fair percentage of government contracts. The SBA monitors government procurement contracts among small businesses, to try to increase the number of contracts, the amount of work contracted, or the amount of money paid that go to small businesses, and how many of those contracts go to certain categories—those owned by women, those owned by "disadvantage", those owned by service-disabled veterans, and those in the HUBZone.

Table 1 *Summary of 2008 and 2009 small business procurement scores at the SBA*

Socio-economic Contracting Achievement for 2009 (%)

	2008 Achievement	2009 Goal	2009 Achievement
Small Business	21.50	23.00	21.89
Women-owned Small Business	3.39	5.00	3.68
Small Disadvantage Business	6.76	5.00	7.57
Service-Disabled Veteran-Owned Small Business	1.49	3.00	1.98
HUBZone	2.34	3.00	2.81

Note. This data refers to information retrieved from http://www.sba.gov.

The SBA's socio-economic program monitors the following concerns: service-disabled veteran-owned, small disadvantaged, women-owned, HUBZone, and 8(a) business development programs. The SBA established a list of small business size requirements to assist companies in determining their small business status. Under Title 13, Code of Federal Regulations, Part 121, the SBA assessed the standards for small companies doing business with the federal government. The SBA annually tracks the status of government procurement from small businesses annually. For example, as noted in Table 1, the SBA surpassed their 2008 achievements; however, in three of five socio-economic groups, the SBA's achievements did not meet 2009 goals.

Some organizations may struggle to find their place in the realm of the small business zone. Minority-owned companies might at times struggle to connect with government organizations.[143] To equalize small business growth in government contracting, the federal government created the Small-Disadvantage Business (SDB) certification program and the Section 8(a) program. These two programs allow minority-owned small businesses to obtain government contracts.

In 2008, the SBA began enforcement of policies governing Small-Disadvantaged businesses. To qualify as a Small-Disadvantaged business, socially or economically disadvantaged individual must 51% or more retain the business. Under the Section 8(a) program, the government contracting agency can distinguish contracts for certified Small-Disadvantaged companies.[170] The SBA provided eight eligibility requirements for Section 8(a) program eligibility, including that the owners have American citizenship, that the business be at least 51% minority-owned, and that the business display an expectation for success.

The federal government developed Microenterprise Development programs (MED) to capitalize on the entrepreneurship of Small-Disadvantaged businesses. The majority of MED businesses are owned by women and/or minorities.[119] Title VII of the Civil Rights Act of 1964 governs minority-owned businesses. Under Title VII, minority-owned businesses may make a disparate-impact civil rights lawsuit if a business practice adversely affects the minority business.[15] Small businesses offer ethnically diverse organizations competitive advantage. Ethnically diverse organizations may increase competition in the small business arena.[168]

Competition in minority owned small businesses enables organizations to segment their strategies to reduce costs and increase profits.[30] Small businesses are imperative to the United States economic growth. Certain groups have either been held back from obtaining government contracts or they find it challenging to navigate the maze that is government contracting. Exclusion of these small businesses, though not specifically bad for the economy, is wrong. As such, the SBA created programs to give particular groups economic advantages. Microenterprise Development programs allow qualified companies to compete as Small-Disadvantaged business.

In 2007, the U. S. Supreme Court updated the rules as applied to Title VII. Based on the court's ruling, Title VII incorporated equal employment practices related to discrimination.[17] The SBA influences the moral attitude of government contracting by offering ethical recommendations to government contracting employees and suppliers. FAR Part 19 includes regulations related to government contracting organizations working with small businesses. To help small businesses understand, and/or register to do business with, government contracting organizations, the SBA provides systems and guidelines: the FAR–Federal Acquisition Regulations; SAM–System for Award Management; FPDS–Federal Procurement Data Systems; GSAM–General Service Administration Manual; and ESRS–Electronic Subcontracting Reporting System.

Competition is a basis for government contracting; however, as previously stated, some organizations find it difficult to obtain these contracts.[85] Employees expect that suppliers will provide services as specified in the contract.[90] Clarity in each contract is essential. If the provisions of the contract are ambiguous, suppliers may apply their own interpretations.

Government contracting employees must offer clearly defined protocols that establish criteria for a contract.[196] FAR Part 19 outlines to each government contracting employee specific rules and regulations associated with government contracting with small companies. On the other side, the SBA, also through FAR, provides guidelines for small businesses working with or wishing to work with a government contracting organization. The regulations and guidelines, however, are useful only if followed, and both sides are rather cavalier about following them.

Government contracting employees may encounter apprehensions and misgivings while administering government contracts. A recurring concern regarding contracting is the integration of contractor priorities with the responsibilities of contract administration.[89] Opportunism may occur in the form of unethical conduct.[113] Employees should monitor a supplier's implementation of the contracting requirements;[90] suppliers may occasionally receive funds yet provide lackluster service.[196]

Another issue regarding contracting-out government services is a lack of oversight.[99] Employees should develop strategies when offering government contracts to private suppliers. To ensure that suppliers provide the goods or service as outlined in the contract, it is important that government contracting employees and suppliers know the requirements of the contract. The lack of accountability and transparency of government outsourcing services may require reforms to the current guidelines regarding the implementation of contracted services.[31] A problem may exist in defining core competencies in government contracting; political and ideological factors may affect core competency decisions.[196]

One of the core competencies for government contracting employees is in knowing the steps needed to deal with customer complaints. Customer service and customer satisfaction are part of contract administration. Ensuring customer satisfaction with all aspects of the contract should be a priority for both the supplier and the government contracting employee. Customers who are unsatisfied with the scope of the contract may submit complaints to supervising authorities. A customer's complaints of ethical violations of the agreement might introduce liquidated damages against the supplier.

Government organizations require ethics when outsourcing contracts. Society expects the previously mentioned organizations to serve the public trust by ensuring that only approved suppliers receive the contracts.[157] Politics may have a bearing on who gets the contract; once that's decided, employees can follow the law in enforcing the contract.[196] Transparency is necessary during the contracting process. Whatever factors influence government contract administration, ensuring that government contracting employees provide suppliers with clearly written contracts is necessary and proper.

Congress retains required and proper authority over the government contracting regulations. Under Article I, Section 8, Clause 18 of the United States Constitution, Congress can delegate powers to the Executive Branch of the federal government. Congressional delegation of authority can change contract management; each branch of the government connects to the other, sometimes making the lines between politics, and public administration blurred.[152] The Executive Branch of the U. S. government established laws central to government contracting organizations and entities. The laws enacted by Congress summarized processes for competitiveness in government contracting.

Competitive sourcing permits public/private companies to do business with federal government organizations.[85] Competition in government contracting authorizes public/private companies to compete with one another to supply goods and services, while affording government organizations opportunities to reduce spending.[193] Competition in government contracting offers incentives to companies to provide the best products and service to the government.

DoD spends billions of dollars each year. Government contracting employees exercise control over billions of dollars. The increase in spending over the past 10 years has provided opportunities for unethical behavior. The greater the value of the contract, the more profit a supplier may receive. There should be prerequisites that guide government contracting employees when administering a large-value contract such as an operational contract.

Members of various branches of the United States military often embark on joint operations globally. These operational units need emergency funds to purchase goods and services needed for the mission. Threats to the national security of the United States afforded Congress the opportunity to establish guidelines for issuing operational contracts. Under a joint-capabilities determination, government contracting organizations use operational contracts to provide goods, services, and support to joint forces of the United States.

Competition should be a prerequisite to satisfactory contract performance.[98] Competition can drive value and efficiency in government contracting. The FAR instructed all government contracting employees to seek out competition prior to issuing government contracts.[29] Knowing the status of a global marketplace may offer suppliers competitive advantages in obtaining contracts.

The proliferation of the Internet with the ability to identify companies electronically surpasses traditional exchanges. Online market research when administering government contracts offer government contracting employees a suitable method of finding relevant suppliers. Market research supports government contracting efforts by providing government contracting employees with the ability to identify and utilize hard-to-find information on business customers and their buying behaviors.

Use of the Internet to conduct market research in government contracting organizations may create a feeling of efficiency. Web sites of companies qualified to conduct business with the government vary significantly. Market research began with an emphasis on finding qualified suppliers to meet government contracting organizations' demand for commercial products, but a rise in government contracting scandals compelled Congress to established government contracting reforms that changed how government contracting employees conduct market research.[121]

With the passage of the Federal Acquisition Streamlining Act of 1994 (FASA) and the Federal Acquisition Reform Act of 1996 (FARA), Congress changed procurement policies for government contracting organizations. The adoption of FASA and FARA enabled government contracting organizations to implement commercial regulations when procuring goods and services.[124] Market research permits government contracting employees to gather information about target markets. Knowing the target market can assist government contracting employees in determining fair and reasonable pricing for government contracts.

Although plans exist to govern the administration of individual contracts, barriers may prevent the government contracting employees from successfully doing their jobs. Barriers to efficient government contracting may emerge through the misunderstanding of market dynamics, government service delivery, or responsibility to society. Government contracting managers may intervene to reduce barriers by conveying to suppliers the improvements required in contractor performance, thereby maximizing the scope of the contract. An additional barrier to efficient government contracting may be limited competition when outsourcing or contracting-out government services.[169] A lack of perceived competition, when contracting-out government services, reduces implementation by government organizations.

Contracting-out government services should provide an economic benefit.[31] Government contracting organizations outsource transportation, garbage collection, janitorial, and other services. Given the heterogeneous nature of these services, it may be economical to contract them out, but only if competition is maintained.[25] As previously stated, competition is the heartbeat of fair government contracting. 10 US Code § 2304 (Contracts: competition requirements) provides that government contracting employees should obtain full and open competition through the use of competitive procedures in accordance with the FAR. Lack of competition provides opportunities for suppliers to offer unfair incentives in return for unauthorized government contracts/awards.

Government contracting employees sometimes administer service contracts with minimal supervision, assigning quality control responsibilities to vendors. Government contracting employees should incorporate the requirements, compliance with the law, and customer satisfaction related to the contract; these services should be conducted ethically.[193]

Federal Acquisition Regulations contain procedures that govern government contracting.[29] OMB Circular A-76 details the processes for contracting-out of goods and services with commercial or private interests. Although employees may encounter barriers to efficient government contracting, they should ethically administer government contracts to authorized suppliers. Money may entice government contracting employees to offer unapproved contracts to unauthorized suppliers. However, government contracting employees should consider their actions and the effect on all stakeholders. A government contracting manager's intervention may or may not be beneficial to controlling barriers in government contract administration.

Civilians/civil servants control large sectors of the government contracting entity. The Federal Procurement Data System – Next Generation [FPDS] revealed that the federal government contracting organizations employ approximately 1.8 million civilians, or 16% of their workforce. Civilian control of some government contracting may strip the organizations of the discipline required to maintain ethical standards.[194] The G.A.O. reported an increase in unwarranted contracts given to suppliers in exchange for cash or for nonmonetary awards. Reports of incidents of mismanagement of public funds have alerted Congress to enact new laws and prompted calls for oversight. But politics, too, may affect the distribution of government contracts. Suppliers may enlist the aid of political proponents to obtain government contracts; political proponents may influence government contracting employees to issue contracts to particular suppliers.

2.6 Political Influence on the Awarding of Government Contracts

Since Congress establishes the rules that direct government contracting, it is easy to believe that politics may influence government contract administration. There are ways to improve governmental contracting ethics through civil-military integration policies, regardless of political affiliation.[5] However, such redistribution of resources can lead to political disagreements rather than practical optimization. Private companies may try to use campaign contributions as bargaining tools to obtain government contracts.

In seeking to understand the impact that corporations and political proponents have on the distribution of government contracts, researchers studied political impact on contract performance. Politics can affect contracting decisions; therefore, the need exists to establish legal frameworks for contract delivery.[90] There should be separation of politics and government contracting, but in fact, politics does influence the dissemination of government contracts.

Why will some suppliers received government contract awards based on their political connections? Private companies seek to determine the awarding of government contracts by contributing to political campaigns. The more financial support an organization contributes to political campaigns, the greater their chance of receiving a government contract.

Political influences might be harmful to the contracting process.[83] Researchers who explored the impact that politics has on contracting employees working overseas found that political control contributed to the misuse of contracting awards and to the incompetence of contract performance.[201]

In the past decade, there has been an increase in the number of politically influenced government contracting arrangements. The government contracts awarded depends on how politically active the business is. Despite the government contracting reforms, suppliers continue to win contracts based on their political contributions. Detecting improper behaviors when administering government contracts may be difficult; however, government authorities have enacted laws and controls to prevent unethical behaviors in government contracting.

2.7 Contract Design

The contract design influences various factors related to awarding the contract to a supplier. Government employees should attempt to create contracts based on government contracting guidelines. Government outsourcing is an essential delivery replacement to improve the effectiveness and flexibility benefits for private and public companies.[184] Government contracting organizations have the task of determining what companies can best offer products and services, and what contract design will be most useful.

In identifying the factors that affect contract design choices, it is necessary to understand government contract design.[91] Contract type and length of the performance can affect contract design decisions.[3] Contract type refers to how the supplier reimburses the government contracting organization. The contract type option determines contract design elements such as effectiveness of contract spending.[3] Government contracting employees use contract design to maintain the relationship between suppliers and government contracting organizations. Government contracts offer valued components in the delivery of goods and services.[109]

There are two contract types in government work: fixed-price and cost-reimbursement; employees are required to know the difference between the two. For each type, guidelines have been published in the FAR and other government contracting regulations. As stated in FAR part 16, fixed-price contracts are non-negotiable, non-adjustable and offer maximum risk and full responsibility for all contract costs to the supplier. When negotiating a fixed-price contract, the supplier agrees to adhere to the contract requirements of a fixed price and delivery within a specified time.[109]

Using a firm-fixed price contract is possible if the government obtains the price for goods or services in advance. When servicing a fixed-price contract, private companies receive fewer profits.[43] Offering fixed-price contracts to suppliers incentivizes the supplier to deliver low-quality outcomes to government contracting organizations. Vendors offering lower prices receive fixed-price contracts. From 1993 through 2008, defense contracting spending doubled from $200 billion to $400 billion.[150] It is unclear why during the same time-frame, government contracting employees reduced the number of fixed-price contracts used and replaced them with cost-reimbursement contracts.

Cost reimbursement contracts ensure suppliers that the government will reimburse the supplier all reasonable costs occurred while executing the contract. Government contracting organizations discourage employees from using cost-reimbursement contracts due to the potential excessive cost to the government.[21] In 2009, Congress passed the American Recovery and Reinvestment Act (ARRA). The ARRA provided that the federal government organization communicate a preference for using fixed-price contracts instead of cost-reimbursement contracts.[137] The Office of Management and Budget (OMB) issued guidance to government contracting organizations regarding the use of cost-reimbursement contracts. Fixed-price contracts offered to suppliers are beneficial to the government contracting organizations because the government can control the costs associated with them. Although cost-reimbursement contracts provide extreme benefits to suppliers, they can offer high cost and low value to the government.

Effective contract liability exists when government contracting agencies understand the prerequisites of contracting guidelines.[108] Government contracting organizations can ensure suppliers' responsibility for implementation of contract requirements. Government contracting organizations use different contract designs. The category of a contract comprises decision-making since the contract affects service and performance.[91] A properly designed contract reduces transaction costs associated with delivering services.[106] The design of each government contract should ensure best value to the government, which is the customer.

Political and economic external forces may push government contracting employees to go outside the scope of the contract, providing opportunities for circumventing legal parameters. When delivering contracts, competition is expected. Competition offers a level of cost control and provides quality delivery of goods and services.

After contract type, length of the contract is the largest influence on performance. The contract period is an agreed time within which to deliver goods or services. Three elements of contract length exist in government contracting: spot market transactions, long-term measures, and contracts that specify a base period but are extendable.[3] Government contracting organizations prefer short-term contracts, since a short-term contract reduces the risk to both the government and the suppliers,[118] but will use long-term contracts if uncertainty exists regarding the outcome of a contract.[3]

The value of the contract results from the contract type and extent. Fixed-price contracts determine the value ex-ante while cost-reimbursement contracts determine the value ex-post. Government contracting organizations can organize each contract to add length and value. If the production of the goods or service is easy, the contract period is shorter. However, if difficulties occur with implementation of the goods and services, the government may extend the agreement to account for previously unknown factors. Government contracting employees should create government contracts to reduce production costs, reduce transaction costs, offer a profit to the supplier, and provide the government with quality goods and services. Different government contracting organizations have experience with administering specific contracts and with suppliers who provide the goods and services as specified in each contract.

2.8 Standards, Guidelines, Compliance, and Regulations

Detailing the standards and guidelines that govern government contracting is essential to employees' understanding the requirements for conducting their jobs ethically. Public service ethics requires that companies establish clear guidelines that conform to a changing global economic request for ethical standards.[1] The Small Business Administration has established guidelines that provide adequate assistance to small businesses competing for government contracts. Organizational standards should govern the company's ethical values.[131] Government contracting employees' lack of adherence to an organization's standard operating procedures may be routine.[167] Inconsistencies in establishing standard operating procedures might be a contributing factor to government contracting employees' inconsistency.

If employees understand how the rules that govern their contracting organizations affect private companies they may find it beneficial to work with those companies to apply government contracting ethical requirements to each company's principles. In an effort to understand how guidelines affect organizational standards, researchers looked at ethical decision making in large organizations such as Enron. Although Enron established ethical standards, employees regularly engaged in unethical behaviors.[203] Unethical behaviors in Enron affected both individuals and stakeholders.[2] Standard operating procedures (SOP) need to be stated clearly; vague guidelines can be worse than none. SOPs provide guidelines for employees to ensure proper completion of the job.[110] A company's standards of conduct should contain the company's ethical guidelines and values.[62] An organization's compliance plan should incorporate ethics.[154] U.S. federal regulations 5 CFR 2635 (Standards of conduct for employees of the executive branch), 41 USC 423 (Procurement Integrity Act), and FAR (Federal Acquisition Regulations) provide guidelines regarding government contracting personnel ethical behavior.

Revisiting compliance and regulations is necessary due to continued unethical behaviors by government contracting employees. To demonstrate ethical behavior when administering government contracts, government employees should recuse themselves from instances that may indicate unethical behaviors.[27] When they do run into unethical behavior, knowing what rules exist will help them in their ethical decision-making.

Conforming to compliance and regulations can be difficult without guidance. Due to continued unethical behaviors, the FAR Council established new ethics regulations that required the creation of written codes of business ethics.[84] Government contracting ethics required augmentation.

Federal Acquisitions Regulation echoes the government contracting compliance rules.[29] Re-engineered subsections of the FAR clarify areas of the original law that seem confusing or unclear.[123] However, timely disclosures of unethical observations in some government contracting organizations remained a problem. Government contracting employees must be able to report unethical behaviors without fear of reprisal.[24] Reprisals, like the original unethical behavior, damage the public trust.

Under Title 48 of the U.S. code of regulations, FAR part 3 prescribes policies and guidelines for avoiding inappropriate business practices and personal conflicts of interest when administering government contracts. It also provides ethics and compliance requirements for individuals doing government contracting business. The Competition in Contracting Act (CICA) allows the GAO to disclose full and complete decision-making requirements in the government contracting.[112] Congress established additional guidelines and regulations to assist government contracting employees when administering government contracts. Government contracting rules and regulations provide tools that may discourage government employees from behaving unethically.

2.9 Other Regulations and Guidance

Statutory authority comes from Congress and provides the legal basis for government contracting. The authority to conduct government contracting comes from public law and executive direction, the authority of the President and federal agencies to issue orders and regulations to enforce the law. Government contracting employees must enforce the regulations of the executive branch.

Numerous guidelines are available to assist the government contracting employee to do their jobs ethically. Federal statute 48 C.F.R. § 37.104(b) prohibits government contracting employees from participating in actions that afford them financial gain. Public servants should show accountability, legality, responsiveness, and integrity when doing their jobs.[48] The American Society for Public Administration (ASPA) code of ethics mandates that government employees deliberate public interest while doing government business.[177] As trust and ethics are essential to government contracting, employees should be sincere from the onset of employment and continue to demonstrate honesty throughout their careers.

Of the laws governing the government contracting process, the following are primary: the Armed Services Procurement Act of 1947 (ASPA), the Federal Property and Administrative Services Act of 1949 (FPASA), the Competition in Contracting Act (CICA), the Federal Acquisition Regulations (FAR), and the Defense Acquisition Regulations Supplement (DFARS). ASPA regulates the acquisition of all property (except land), construction, and services by defense agencies.

As noted under 10. U.S.C. 2307 (Contract financing), government contracting employees, may reimburse suppliers for services rendered under a government contract. Subpart 32.1 of the FAR notes that government contracting employees can create additional payments to suppliers for execution of contracts, but the payments cannot exceed the negotiated price of the contract. In 1949, with the enactment of the Federal Property and Administrative Services Act of 1949 (FPASA), the General Services Administration was established. FPASA regulates procurement, utilization, and disposal of government property. CICA regulates both defense and civilian purchases and mandates that all government contracting entities will provide full and open competition prior to seeking sole-source acquisitions.

CICA directed that all contracting actions terminate if a vendor disputes any provision of the contract through a GAO protest. The FAR is the primary regulation in the Federal Acquisition System, and the DFARS are supplemental documents to the FAR specifically structured for agencies in the Department of Defense (DoD). The FAR and DFARS contain regulatory and policy guidelines for implementation of government contracting functions. In addition to the principal laws, Congress generated supplementary laws that the government contracting employees may not use on a daily basis; however, the regulations may be necessary for particular aspects of government contract administration. Congress enacted the Federal Acquisition Streamlining Act of 1994 (FASA) in an attempt to reform government contracting business.[124] With the implementation of the FASA and the Federal Acquisition Reform Act of 1996 (FARA), Congress emphasized the use of market research for the government agencies.

FASA and FARA detail the federal government's preferences for the acquisition of commercial items. The FASA and the FARA provided government contracting organizations with direction and authority to consider the cost of buying products and services from private suppliers. Federal government organizations are dependent on contracting services to purchase goods and services. Over-reliance on outsourcing led to scandals and public outcry for reform of government contracting policies.

Enactment of regulatory policies provided simplification of aggressive policies for government contracting organizations when buying from commercial suppliers. The purpose of FASA and FARA is to eliminate corruption and excessive cost in government contracting by focusing on competition. Adding competition to government contracting purchasing decisions might improve efficiency since competition causes suppliers to consider all aspects of the contract. The imposition of FASA and FARA revised more than 225 statutory regulations related to government contracting procurement, offering rules to ensure employees' compliance with established laws and, hopefully, to help them understand the necessity for ethical behavior when conducting government business.

3

QUALITATIVE CASE STUDY RESEARCH

A case study is an implementation of a research method
involving an up-close, in-depth, and detailed examination
of a subject of study (the case), as well as its related
contextual conditions.[239]

3.1 Introduction - A Qualitative Case

In Section 3, I have provided a summary of the research components
and explored government contracting employees' insights regarding
the knowledge required to prevent unethical behaviors by government
contracting employees. This section also covers (a) the intention of the
doctoral study, (b) participants in the study, (c) research method and
design, (d) population of the research, (e) data collection, and analysis
techniques, (f) ethical research, and finally, (g) reliability and validity of
the research process.

3.2 Purpose Statement

As previous stated the purpose of this qualitative case study was to provide a clear understanding of the knowledge required by managers to mitigate unethical behaviors of their employees when administering contracts. This case study, supported by the research of Bao, Wang, Larsen, and Morgan, formed the basis for researching and understanding the worth of management and leadership development in government contracting.[11] Twenty-one government contracting managers from a defense organization in the mid-Atlantic region shared their insights about the strategies needed to stop government contracting employees' unethical behaviors. This study might affect a business practice by helping government contracting managers learn strategies to reduce employees' unethical behaviors.

3.3 Role of the Researcher

I was the data collection instrument. The instrument is the researcher who critically collects data and ensures that the information represents what participants are conveying.[141] My dual role of researcher and business member presented both opportunities and challenges for this doctoral study. Having familiarity with the organization and access to information pertinent to this study did not prevent challenges in mitigating personal bias. Challenges that may be prominent when researching a specific population include engaging with participants, translating data, participant recruitment, data collection, and reliability. Establishing relationships with interviewees offered a broader perspective of the targeted culture.

In-depth interviews were the chosen method to collect data for this research study. The qualitative researcher analyzes and interprets the data by presenting the value throughout the interview process.[185] A qualitative researcher should commit to the common good, eliminate bias, establish clear distinctions between the researcher and the research subject, and step out of his or her comfort zone. The qualitative researcher should incorporate participants' feedback into the study.[158] In this study, the goals were to gather and present each participant's knowledge in a reasonable and equitable manner. It is necessary to reduce the effects of personal beliefs and biases, and to possess the logical and cognitive skills needed to do so. The researcher notes the study environment in anticipation of challenges participants may encounter.

For this study, the technique employed under McCormack's lenses provided a flexible structure for analysis of multifaceted data. Drawing on an individual's experience and presenting their story in an unbiased manner proved beneficial, as well as being essential to the research process. The qualitative researcher should be knowledgeable about principles, practice, dialog, and the relevance of the research subject.[116] The principles of the Belmont Report stressed protection of individual's personal information.[61] The goal was to ensure that I offered integrity by ensuring that participants' information remained protected.

3.4 Participants

This qualitative research study involved interviews with government contracting managers in Pay Grades GS-11 to GS-13. As a government contracting employee working in the mid-Atlantic region, I had access to government contracting managers in the chosen geographic area and had no need for snowball sampling (i.e. participants' referring other potential candidates). Each participant received an invitation that explained the purpose and intent of the study along with a blanket consent form. The consent form contained a statement that participation in this study was optional and that declining to participate in the study could occur at any time. The names of individuals would remain confidential. An individual's experience would determine their participation in this study.

Obtaining consent to participate in sensitive research studies can be difficult.[49] Privacy and the security of participants' information is a priority.[70] Protecting participants from harm by obtaining informed consent ensures each participant's right to privacy. The nature of this proposed research study might be sensitive, as it involved obtaining information from government contracting managers. Universities may require their researchers conducting interviews with potentially vulnerable groups to get permission to conduct the research study. I asked for and received permission from an authorizing official from the participation organization. Each participant received an identifier such as P1, P2, or P3. During the interview process, some participants added information to the interview subject. All study data including interview transcripts and analysis information will remain secure for a five-year period. After the five-year period, I will permanently destroy the study data by shredding all paper copies and writing over any electronic records. Ensuring the privacy and comfort of government contracting managers established ease with sharing information.

3.5 Research Method and Design

Academic strategies may employ an exclusively qualitative or quantitative method, or a mixed method research design that combines qualitative and quantitative data into the same plan.[67] A qualitative methodology and case study research design led this research study. Using elements of qualitative research provided benefit to this study by including rigorous data collection from in-depth, semistructured interviews.[44] Using semistructured interviews facilitated obtaining real-world information from participants in Pay Grades GS-11 to GS-13.

3.5.1 Method

The qualitative research method allows researchers to describe naturally occurring phenomenon through pragmatic assumptions, interpretive analysis, and ideological commitments.[74] Quantitative research links scientific investigation with measurable relationships between variables based on statistical interpretations and conceptual arguments.[96] The qualitative research process allows for consideration of questions based on participants' characterization of real-world events and offers insight into a phenomenon.[9] The problem considered influences the methods employed in the research study.[73] The qualitative research process comprises a practical application of predetermined questions to get the perspectives of a small group of participants regarding their experiences.[140] Conducting semistructured interviews allowed participants to provide additional information to enrich the research subject.

Quantitative data provides identification and categorization of participants' perceptions. The quantitative process entails using theories, statistical analysis, and hypothesis from which to draw a conclusion.[96] This research does not require statistical data analysis; therefore, it does not meet the criteria for a quantitative study.[59] Using a quantitative approach may prevent researchers from replicating this study. Quantitative researchers might fail to grasp the complexity and essence of the information participants of the study.[92] A qualitative research method is an evidenced-based approach that allows understanding a situation from the participant's perspective.[176] Since a mixed method employs both qualitative and quantitative methods, it is not suited for this study.

3.5.2 Research Design

Some researchers prefer qualitative case study designs to address issues regarding social, organizational, and institutional effects in individual organizations or groups and to promote change or improve practice.[124] Understanding the phenomenon of why government contracting managers lack knowledge of how to prevent unethical behaviors by government contracting employees is vital to preventing future unethical behaviors. Principal research designs for qualitative studies include case study, narrative study, ethnography, grounded theory, and phenomenology.[181] The research question shapes the research design.[42] Considering all of these, the research design most appropriate for this study was a single case study. The foundation of case study research is the study of human experience and the direction of human awareness towards that experience.[140] Choosing a research design that allowed understanding of participants' perspectives was important in finding answers to the research question.

When related literature is limited, a case study proves useful for gathering data.[199] The case study design justified the research question by helping me to specify two purposes. The research question helped me to articulate the relationship between the goal for this study and the conceptual framework, as well as giving credence to the relationship between methods and validity of the study.[114] This case study design will allow focus on the process within one organization during a short time frame. The result of this study offered the emphasis on the process rather than the outcome and holistic view of the issue rather than isolated factors.

Of the other designs mentioned, none suited this research as well as a case study. Although a phenomenological design relies primarily on participant interviews, the researcher does not focus on one individual or group.[77] Narrative research shares similar traits with the case study; however, narrative research is time-consuming.[92] Ethnographic qualitative research that focuses on collecting data from a particular culture or sharing group did not suit this study; the process is also timely and costly.[126] Grounded theory research was not suitable because grounded theory does not require a fixed time for concluding the study; grounded theory can be never-ending.[81] Case study describes a current circumstance, is multifaceted and can provide different answers to complex problems.[164]

3.6 Population and Sampling

The population of this research study consisted of government contracting individuals. The target sample was a purposeful selection of government contracting personnel in Pay Grades GS-11 to GS-13.

A qualitative researcher embraces purposeful sampling.[175] Using purposeful sampling in qualitative research allows the researcher to capture an in-depth understanding of participants' information that is not available from random sampling.[146] Purposeful sampling provides for the separation of individuals based on qualification criteria.[135] Researchers have used purposeful sampling to analyze the behavior and moral development at the U.S. Military Academy at West Point, and to consider an ethical environment in nursing. Using a purposeful sampling allows researchers to gain perspectives from a vast distribution of subject matter experts.

A qualitative researcher uses purposeful sampling to select participants based on experience and nuanced understanding.[93] Purposeful sampling was the desired method of selecting government contracting managers to participate in the semistructured interviews. Using a purposeful sampling to deliberate government managers' insights regarding unethical behavior when administering government contracts, suited this study. When using purposeful sampling, the qualitative researcher should decide the demographics and number of participants sampled as well as the sampling method used.[50] To be a part of this study, participants were government contracting managers in Pay Grades GS-11 through GS-13. They needed to be involved in managing government contracting, and willing to participate in the study.[120] Sample size and geographical area provided adequate control over the evaluation process.[28]

Qualitative research studies typically have smaller sample sizes. When there is no further information and redundancy is evident, the researcher obtains saturation.[189] Determining saturation in this qualitative research study aided in getting an adequate sample size of participants.[133] In this research process, I reached saturation when redundancy occurred, and I gained no additional data. If the population is too large or varies significantly, the information given might be overwhelming.[46] A minimum of 20 participants appeared to be an adequate sample size for conducting this research study. Twenty-one individuals suited this study. As a result, the information was richer and more detailed than if more people had participated. A sample size of 21 government contracting managers proved an adequate population of experiences to analyze the research data adequately and find themes of understanding. In addition, although this study cannot be replicated, ensuring that sufficient data is available to continue this study may be an important aspect to justifying this study.[199] Since future researchers may not have access to the same participants or data, the results might differ. Therefore, the goal for this study was to produce research that could inform readers and augment their understanding of the subject of ethical behaviors in government contracting.

3.7 Ethical Research

The qualitative researcher should address ethical challenges prior to conducting the study.[75] Respect for autonomy, kindness, and impartiality may alleviate problems caused by ethical issues.[64] Ethical research emphasizes the integrity of the researcher and highlights the tensions between participation and the rigor of the study.[130] Quality in this doctoral study involved the capability to complete an Internal Review Board (IRB) approval process.

Certification of training from the National Institutes of Health (NIH) was a necessary step in obtaining an approved doctoral project. A university's Office of Research Ethics and Compliance approved this research proposal prior to data collection. After approval from the IRB, I notified each study participant of the doctoral process. I notified potential participants using e-mail, phone, or direct contact prior to the interview process. Each participant received an invitation to participate in the study along with the consent form. The consent form stated that participation in the study was optional and reiterated that participants received no compensation for participating.[186] Participants reviewed, asked questions for clarity, and signed the consent form stating understanding of all parameters.

Ethically, it was important to obtain permission to conduct the study because I was required to prove adherence to provisions for protecting human subjects and permission to use the interview instrument obtained. To ensure participants' privacy and to conduct the interviews uninterrupted, I arranged sit-down time both face-to-face and via telephone with each person away from the workplace. Out of respect for privacy, individual's names will not appear in the doctoral study. Individuals will receive unique identifiers of P1 through P21 and E1 through E8. I notified individuals regarding their right to withdraw for the interviews at any time without penalty. At the end of the discussions, participants reviewed a copy of their interview transcripts for accuracy and noted any changes. I will keep all research data including written, audio and electronic securely for a five-year period after which the data will be shredded or electronically written over.

3.8 Data Collection

How the researcher gathers data may affect individuals' willingness to participate in the research study.[32] Engaging participants in multidisciplinary dialogs may bring richness to the conversation for both researcher and participant. The goal is to engage participants in a comprehensive dialog while mitigating personal bias during the interview process.

3.8.1 Instruments

As previously stated, I was the data collection instrument. The researcher as the data collection instrument constructs ideas from data presented during the interview process.[141] The goal for data collection in this study was to gather information related to government contracting managers' knowledge of how to prevent unethical behaviors by government contracting employees. Additional goals were to provide enhanced description of the results of the interviews that might assist the government organization to implement best practices and process improvements regarding ethical requirements when administering contracts. Interviews were the primary method of data collection in this doctoral study. Open-ended, semistructured interview questions facilitated the understanding of the phenomenon captured in the following question: What knowledge do government contracting managers need to mitigate unethical behaviors of government contracting employees when administering contracts? An open-ended, semistructured interview format provides the qualitative researcher the opportunity to obtain in-depth answers from personal questions.[198]

In this case study, 21 mid-level managers participated in semistructured interviews directly related to the study topic. Potential weakness of this interview method involved interviewer bias and response bias. Strengths of this method included onsite access to participants and the opportunity to gain a clear understanding of contextual indications. Case study was made more accurate and credible by using multiple data collection sources.[199] Data collection included interviews and documents such as prior case studies and government reports.

When using interviews as a data collection instrument, the researcher should ensure that the interviews provide substance to the research study.[188] The qualitative researcher should move from a one-dimensional view, embracing the insights of participants as given in interviews.[182] Researchers have used semistructured interviews to explore the interaction between ethics and methodological innovation in qualitative research. It has been noted that the venue for conducting interviews is as important as the interview instrument. Consideration of sensitivities to public exposure and participant confidentiality are critical to successful interviews.[130] One researcher compared participants and researchers' interactions using semistructured telephone and face-to-face interviews. The researcher found no major difference in participants' interactions with the researcher based on the type of interview used; however, the environment contributed to determining the best mode for conducting the interviews.

The comfort level of participants determined the interview venue. Documentation of participants' responses from the interviews ensured reliability of the data.[197] Reliability in qualitative research correlates with an approximation of the sample, time, and participants' accounts.[128] I transcribed participants' interview responses on interview instruments located in a secured folder on my personal computer using Microsoft Word.

3.8.2 Data Collection Technique

In a qualitative research design, the researcher collects information through observations, documentation, and interviews.[111] Participants knew the researcher and felt confident that the researcher would protect their privacy. A researcher should prepare and carefully plan for the interview process, and then focus on the interviewee and allow the individual to present details useful to the interview process.

Semistructured interviews and prior documentation were the data collection method used in this qualitative doctoral study. Discussions using eight semistructured interview questions comprised the interview process, the interview taking place at mutually agreed-upon locations. The qualitative exploration of this study assessed the factors that might contribute to unethical behaviors by government contracting employees and the knowledge that participants might have to help managers in reducing employees' unethical behaviors.

After transcribing the data, I used member checking to confirm the accuracy of my understanding of participants' data and to ensure accurate representation of participants' information. Participants used member checking to review the study data to determine whether or not I had portrayed their information accurately. Participants received appropriate sections of the research report and offered comments on accuracy of my interpretations. Using member checking allowed me to focus on the content of participants' experiences and request comment on participants' review. Transcription of interviews and member checking established the validity of the research data by confirming what participants, government contracting employees who were experts at acquiring goods and services for the benefit of government entities, intended to say. Organizing the data into manageable files also helped with validity of the study.

3.8.3 Data Organization Techniques

Data coding consisted of analyzing information from participants' interviews and transforming that information into a form understandable by Ethnograph v6 software. Data management involved deciding the most efficient data organization technique to use. Preserving participants' data electronically and non-electronically increased the effectiveness of the data analysis. Data organization techniques included creating an electronic journal, placing responses in the order of interviews, and electronically storing data in a folder called *Participants' Information*. To ensure privacy, each participant received identifiers of P1, P2, P3, and so on.[37] I transcribed the data into a Word document and pasted the transcribed information into Ethnograph v6 software. The privacy and confidentiality of the research data will be protected for five years, after which, the data will be destroyed.

3.9 Data Analysis Technique

When member checking was complete, and clarifications made, I began data analysis. Qualitative data analysis techniques involve reducing data into themes or categories. The Ethnograph v6 computer software package used in data analysis proved beneficial in analyzing raw data collected from the semistructured interviews, by marking the data with the specific identifiers assigned to interview participants.

The recommendations of qualitative methodology provided the basis for this study because this study did not require hypothesis testing or statistical interpretations. I focused on obtaining meaningful characterization of real-world events. To start the data analysis process, I asked each participant eight open-ended questions. After copying the research data into Microsoft

Word, I used the software in data analysis. Upon loading the data in the Ethnograph v6 software, the search for common themes ensued. This process provided a systematic manner for coding data into key themes. Inductive coding can be used to gather information related to different research studies. Inductive coding can be used to explore the relationship between leaders and student participation. Key themes emerged when I used inductive coding in the data analysis process.

3.10 Reliability and Validity

Addressing reliability and validity helped in achieving verification of this research study. To ensure the reliability and validity of the research, I searched for logical conclusions based on the analyzed data. In this study, I assessed the validity in relation to the purpose of the research study and participants' perspectives.

3.10.1 Reliability

Reliability of this study was an essential objective. Reliability in research addresses the ability of other researchers to apply results of a previous study to a broader group other than those who participated in the study. In other words, would similar results be obtained if other researchers applied the same set of data to different groups of participants? Reliability in qualitative research emphasizes the nonexistence of careless errors and presents the research as raw data.[200] Protecting the integrity, quality, and reliability of the research data was a key focus of the study. Documentation of all aspects of assessment established reliability and credibility of the data. Reliability in qualitative research depends on an accurate representation of research participants' perspectives and the link to the research question.[86] A necessary step in validating a coding scheme in qualitative research entails the use of intercoders.[22] Intercoder reliability can be a key component of the qualitative data analysis process.

3.10.2 Validity

Researchers use validity in qualitative research to verify the authenticity of the study.[93] The qualitative researcher uses validity to outline the relationship between the research design and the data interpretations.[95] High validity strengthens the trustworthiness of the research tools. In this case study, measurement of validity occurred through techniques such as member checking, triangulation, and data saturation.

As in reliability, using member checking provided grounds for data validation. Ensuring that each participant reviewed a copy of their interview transcript for accuracy served to validate the data. Member checking or respondent validation improves the accuracy and validity of this study. As previously stated, using member checking allowed participants to verify findings, provide feedback, and provide further insights beneficial to this study. Summarizing the data and obtaining participants' feedbacks, corrections, and additional insights provided clarity in the final data analysis. Allowing each participant to review a copy of his or her transcript offered further validity to this study. This review promoted affirmation, feedback, critique, and cooperation.

Embracing triangulation throughout the validation phase of the research process helped in mitigating bias. Methodological triangulation from interviews and documentation strengthened the validity of this study. Data triangulation supports the validity of a case study. Methodological triangulation from interviews and exploration of documents related to the research subject identified similarities and differences in current responses and past observances. My objective in this study was to use data triangulation to promote the completeness of the data collection and classify emerging findings.

Data saturation occurred when no new themes emerged, and coding became routine. Although I reached the saturation point after 16 interviews, I continued to interview participants until I conducted 21 semistructured interviews.

As we know, qualitative studies contain limitations. Although there were themes to support the research question, this study may be limited and presents opportunities for future research. The inability to study all managers in government contracting presents further limits on this study. However, information gathered through the interview process, document inquiry, and data analysis should be transferability to members of the contracting community.

4

ETHICAL IMPLEMENTATION OF GOVERNMENT CONTRACTING – THE MANAGERS' VIEWPOINT

The government contracting manager must have a solid understanding of statutory and regulatory rules that govern federal contracting. This position requires an individual who has in-depth knowledge of the various aspects of US federal government contracting to include proposal development; negotiations, administration, and contract close-out. The government contracting manager will administer contracts and develop/maintain business relationships at the project and program level. This individual will implement contracting strategies, answer questions on the operational aspects of contracting and specific contract management aspects pertaining to the programs assigned; contribute to new and innovative business and contracting solutions; support business planning activities. [National Contract Management Association. (2015, January). *Federal Contracts Manager*. Retrieved from: ncmajobs.com]

4.1 Introduction – Managers Views

Government contracting managers are required not only to assign duties to their employees but to *develop* their employees. Anyone can manage anything; however, the individual who can motivate their employees to do the right thing is a *Leader*.

4.2 Overview of Study

The purpose of this qualitative case study was to provide a clear understanding of the knowledge required by government contracting managers to regulate ethical behaviors of government contracting employees. To comprehend the government contracting managers' understanding, I established one research question and eight supporting interview questions. The questions structure the presentation of my findings later in this chapter. I discussed applications to professional practice, implications for social change, made recommendations for action, as well as recommendations for further study.

This section begins with an overview of the analysis of the knowledge that federal government contracting managers require for the job of regulating unethical behaviors by those they manage and a presentation of the study's findings. One research question comprised the study: What knowledge do government contracting managers need to regulate unethical behaviors of government contracting employees when administering contracts? I conducted semi-structured interviews with 21 government contracting managers. The findings from the data analysis revealed evidence that training and communication are central to managing government contracting employees' unethical behaviors. Government contracting focuses on customer service. Good customer service benefits all stakeholders; bad customer service promotes negativity.

Data collection included 21 semistructured interviews and company documents pertaining to ethical requirements of government contracting. Company documents as well as the interviews provided methodological triangulation of the data. I analyzed the data and discovered four emerging themes. The themes related to organizational strategic guidelines as described in the company documents. The four themes were (a) the need for continued training in ethics, (b) the necessity of trust, (c) the adequacy or inadequacy, to current training or to required training, and (d) the benefits of ethical government contracting. The findings from the data analysis revealed evidence that supported the conclusion that training and communication are central to managing government contracting employees' unethical behaviors.

4.3 Presentation of the Findings

Since September 2011, government contracting has changed. The war on terrorism has reinforced the realization that business can no longer be "business as usual." The goal of government contracting in the 21st century is to strengthen the industrial base, promote competition, and be more cost effective. Government contracting has a goal of *better buying power*. Better buying power focuses on continued improvements in defense acquisition. *Yes*, improvements cost money; however, that cost cannot be at the expense of the taxpayer. Spending taxpayer dollars wisely must be a goal of government contracting employees. Government contracting managers require the tools to teach their employees the ethical goals of government contracting.

The findings from data analysis presented pertain to the central research question: What knowledge do government contracting managers need to mitigate unethical behaviors of government contracting employees when administering contracts? Framed by the stakeholder theory, a qualitative case study was designed and purposeful sampling used which resulted in 21 government contracting managers answering eight open-ended questions regarding contracting managers' understanding of the knowledge required to diminish unethical behaviors by government contracting employees. I analyzed participants' responses from face-to-face interviews and company documents using Ethnograph v6 software to assist in establishing the findings.

The sample came from a group of managers at a government contracting organization in the mid-Atlantic area of the United States. Based on the interview questions, participants presented responses that varied in scope, depth, and consideration. All of the individuals approached agreed to participate in the study, a response rate of 100%. Based on Dibley's assessment of McCormack's Lens, I drew on each participant's experience to develop and present the research findings in an unbiased manner. Although I used the questions to direct each interview, an open-ended approach guided the interview process.

The conceptual framework for this research study was stakeholder theory. The concept of stakeholder theory that encourages business managers to consider the principles of organizational and public ethics when determining business compliance was supported by much of the interview responses and reiterated by the company documents.[67] Themes emerged which demonstrated similarities and differences amongst participants. Themes in qualitative research emerge from patterns not predetermined.[73] Qualitative researchers focus on new patterns, themes, or information that provides new insight into a specific subject. The four emerging themes reflected vital results of this study and represented more than 80% of the responses in each category.

4.3.1 The Need for Continued Training in Ethics.

In regards to training or development methods managers used to guide government contracting employees to administer contracts ethically, 38% of participants relied on established policies and guidance while 52% assessed that regular training was key (see Table 2). As noted by 11 participants, annual training plays a vital role in ensuring that any changes in organizational policies are clearly outlined. Findings from this study enforce the assessment that incorporating government contracting requirements, compliance with the law, and customer satisfaction encourages ethical behaviors.[193]

Participants posited that training government contracting employees on the fundamentals of the FAR, DFARS, and local ethical guidance presented further opportunities for employees to understand the requirements of doing their jobs ethically. Formal ethics training encourages ethical organizational development; therefore, may decrease instances of unethical behaviors.[191] In addition, five percent of participants stated that open communication presents further opportunities for presenting ethical training and development to government contracting employees. Another 5% of participants posited that managers of government contracting employees must lead by example.

Table 2 *Nodes Related to Theme 1 - Frequency of Themes for Ethics Requires Continued Training*

Theme	n	% of frequency of occurrence
Clarity is needed in regard to organizational standards	14	66%
FAR, DFARS, local policies	13	62%
Training/development methods used - regular/continued training	11	52%
No problems with implementing organizational standards	10	48%
Training/development methods used - established policies	8	38%
Improvement in ethical policies	6	29%
Communicating organizational policies proved challenging	5	24%
Problems balancing urgency of need with quality	3	14%

Note: n=frequency

Different managers have different styles, views, and ideas. In fact, participants noted various fundamental ways in which to address employees' understanding of ethical requirements. However, the majority of participants, 62%, relied on policies and guidance such as the FAR, DFARS, and local policies to guide employees to do their jobs ethically. Participants posited that communication is vital to clearly presenting fundamentals needed by employees (see Table 2).

Forty-eight percent of participants indicated no problems in implementing the organization leaders' policies. These participants maintained that leading by example and clearly communicating the organization's philosophies appeared important to employees' understanding and implementation of those policies. However, 24% of participants stated that communicating the organization's policies seemed challenging because the policies were at times unclear (see Table

2). Findings from this study discount researchers' findings that managers willingly manipulate regulatory policies to ensure that cases of unethical behaviors dissipate[152a]. Responsible leaders can influence their employees ethically. Notwithstanding, P17 posited that the organizational policies are subject to individual interpretation. P8 assessed that the policies constantly change and that the guidelines offered appear contradictory or confusing to the employees.

When asked how the participants could overcome the challenges presented, 66% (see Table 2) posited that being able to understand the organization's policies and not offering personal interpretations could be helpful in clearly communicating the philosophies to their government contracting employees. The managers maintained that the policies written in legal language are challenging to interpret and present to the government contracting employee. Another issue that 14% of participants presented was that helping government contracting employees to balance urgency of need with attaining quality of service made implementing the organization leaders' policies and philosophies challenging. Organizations in the public arena are expected to retain desirable traits of public trust, resource administration, and good governance.

The theme associated with *ethics requires continued training* included the answers related to understanding the requirements needed to mitigate the government contracting employees' unethical behaviors. The patterns found in participants' responses included words that referred to (a) maintaining required training, (b) providing relevant training, (c) ensuring that regulations are clear and concise, and (d) communicating ethical guidelines to government contracting employees.

4.3.2 The Necessity of Trust.

Participants' views varied based on their experience and beliefs. Fifty-two percent of participants indicated that they had not faced unethical behaviors with their employees administering government contracts. Some managers addressed issues encountered. For example, 14% assessed that unethical vendors caused employees to behave unethically (see Table 3). The participants maintained that if unethical vendors did not approach employees and offer money for contracts, employees might not have a reason to administer contracts unethically.

Table 3 *Nodes Related to Theme 2 - Frequency of Themes for Trust is Vital*

Theme	n	% of frequency of occurrence
Honesty, integrity is representative of organizational philosophy	8	38%
Communication	5	24%
Unethical vendors	3	14%
Individual Beliefs	2	10%
Training used in employees' development	2	10%
D1: Director's Guidance - Engage with employees, customers, and stakeholders	3	100%

Note: n=frequency

Ten percent of participants posited that individual beliefs drive ethical/unethical behaviors. These managers affirmed the assessment that public servants must show accountability, legality, responsiveness, and integrity when doing their jobs. The managers posited that an individual of high ethical standards would not cooperate with unethical vendors presenting money for favors, but would administer contracts based on the ethical standards set forth in government contracting guidance. Twenty-four percent of participants confirmed the organizational director's guidance (see Table 3) that communication is vital to ensuring that government contracting employees understand the ethical guidelines and the ramifications of going outside the scope of established policies. Participants' responses varied based on the type of employees they managed.

A small minority, 10%, maintained that more than any other factors, using training to develop government contracting employees might affect employees' ethical understanding of government contracting administration. The bulk of participants looked at the organization's philosophies and combined them with their personal beliefs when addressing unethical behaviors in government contracting employees. Moral judgments pose substantial challenges to individual and organizational integrity.[213] Thirty-eight percent of participants posited that honesty and integrity represented their organization's primary philosophy.

Government contracting organizations' mission is to support the warfighter by offering value-added supplies and services at a fair and reasonable price while keeping in mind the philosophy of honesty and integrity, above all else. Participants posited that open communications allowed employees to document and report unethical behaviors encountered. Participants stated that leading by example was a primary factor for mitigating government contracting ethical behaviors. If the employee understood the organization's philosophy and believed in the manager's willingness to enforce the policies, the employee might be willing to follow the required ethical guidelines.

Themes included those questions related to participants' perceptions of issues managers may face regarding the knowledge needed to diminish unethical behaviors of government contracting employees. The answers belonging to the theme *trust is vital* contained patterns based on participants' responses such as *honesty, integrity,* and *ethics*. The categories of significance in the responses included: *integrity* with six responses, *honesty* with four responses, and *ethics* with three responses, thus demonstrating the relevance that the category had on participants. The category related to *trust is vital* included participants' responses reflecting that values, trust, and morals must guide ethical behaviors.

4.3.3 The Adequacy or Inadequacy, to Current Training or to Required Training.

Thirty-eight percent of participants assessed that the training offered provided government contracting employees with adequate discipline needed to do their jobs ethically (see Table 4). While those managers determined no improvements were needed, 29% of participants posited that training must be relevant to the work government contracting employees do. Participants confirmed the assessment that formal ethics training encourages ethical organizational development and decreases instances of unethical behaviors. P4 assessed that training must be tailored to each government contracting activity. The managers suggested that sometimes training offered by the organization differed from the scope of work employees do therefore making the training appear irrelevant.

Table 4 *Nodes Related to Theme 4 - Frequency of Themes for Adequacy of Training*

Theme	n	% of frequency of occurrence
Current training is sufficient	8	38%
Training must be relevant	6	29%

Note: n=frequency

Ensuring that adequate training is presented to government contracting employees is vital to sustaining an ethical workforce. With only 38% of managers agreeing that training offer is sufficient, I recommend that relevant, reoccurring training be offered to current and future government contracting employees. Relevant training can provide the government contracting workforce with the ability to conduct self-assessments related to government contracting ethical requirements. Managers also confirmed the belief that organizational ethics training is critical to effectively presenting an ethical culture within the organization. P2 and P4 posited that training must be relevant and comply with established regulations.

4.3.4 The Benefits of Ethical Government Contracting.

Participants stressed the benefits of mitigating government contracting employees' unethical behaviors. Benefits included (a) improvements to customer service, (b) cost savings, (c) boosting consumer confidence in government contracting organizations, (d) self-satisfaction, and (e) improvement in workforce performance. The managers agreed that it was beneficial for government contracting employees to do their jobs ethically. Overwhelmingly, as noted in Table 5, 76% of participants assessed cost savings as a major benefit. P5 noted an effective use of taxpayer dollars, while P11 posited that knowing that taxpayer's money is spent ethically may benefit society. Whether cost savings to the government, customer or the public, participants affirmed organizational director's guidance (see Table 5) that saving money benefits all stakeholders.

Results from this study confirm previous findings that focusing on the broader area of stakeholder management and social responsibility enhancements ethical compliance within government contracting. Thirty-five percent of participants noted other potential benefits (see table 5) including improvements in customer service, boosting consumer confidence, and improvement to the workforce, and 19% noted self-satisfaction. As noted within the conceptual framework of this study, changes to the government contracting policies can benefit all stakeholders. Incorporating ethics with organizational strategies benefits not only the organization but also all stakeholders.[67]

Table 5 *Nodes Related to Benefits of Ethical Government Contracting*

Theme	n	% of frequency of occurrence
Current training is sufficient	8	38%
Training must be relevant	6	29%
D2: Director's Guidance - Achieve price reductions across organization	1	100%

Note: n=frequency

Participants confirmed the assessment that customer service and customer satisfaction encompass the administration of government contracts. Matching organization and customer values can produce a customer-centric environment.[129]

4.3.5 Particular Situations

The category related to *trust is vital* addressed ideas regulated by principles or values that apply to situations requiring contextual judgments.

The patterns found in participants' responses included words such as (a) *document and reported,* (b) *communicate,* (c) *zero tolerance, and* (d) *encourage positive behaviors,* addressing how particular situations could influence ethical behaviors and decisions. Participants noted *integrity* as a behavior that comprises the individuals' responsibility for his/her actions or a thought as a whole is part of an ethical behavior. The category related to *ethics requires continued training* addressed ideas related to regulations, guidance, or law. Participants' responses included phrases such as *FAR/ DFARS is a must, regular training must be conducted, relevant training is needed, maintain current training,* and *clarify policies.* Participants posited that making guidelines and regulations clear could assist government contracting managers to clarify ethical guidelines to government contracting employees.

5

ETHICAL IMPLEMENTATION OF GOVERNMENT CONTRACTING – THE EMPLOYEES' PERSPECTIVE

An Employee is an individual hired to do a specific job. An Employee barters his or her skills, knowledge, experience, and contribution in exchange for compensation from an employer – HumanResources.com

A person who has agreed by contract to perform specified legal services for an employer in exchange for money. – Duhaime's Law Dictionary

5.1 Introduction – What About Us? The Employees' Perspective

Society lavishes attention on corruption, commonly referred to as the misuse of public position for private gain. The misuse of public position and power at the expense of citizens remain a problem in government contracting organizations. This abuse takes many forms, from receiving direct payments for unauthorized contracts to channeling public monies inappropriately to enrich oneself. Previous studies investigated corruption in government contracting but no study was found that determine how to combat the corruption.

Considering government contracting managers' perspective on what is needed to moderate their employees' unethical behaviors is beneficial to the managers; however, understanding the employees' needs can similarly enhance the understanding of what is needed to deter unethical behaviors. This section contains the results of an analysis of the employees' understanding of the requirements needed to diminish unethical behaviors.

5.2 Overview

The purpose of this follow-on assessment was to provide a clear understanding of government contracting employees' understanding of the requirements needed to mitigate unethical behaviors. To compare and contrast government contracting employees' knowledge with that of their managers, I created 8 comparative interview questions aimed at seeing the process from each employee's perspective. I distributed surveys to 8 government contracting employees. The findings from the data analysis revealed (a) government contracting employees' lack of understanding of the ethical requirement process, (b) the need for training is to reduce unethical behavior, and (c) the need for additional communication between employees and management. As previously stated, the focus of government contracting is good customer service. Good customer service can benefit all stakeholders while negative customer service promotes pessimism. Data collected included answers to 8 survey questions. The survey questions provided data triangulation when used in conjunction with previous semistructured interviews and company documents pertaining to ethical requirements of doing government contracting.

5.3 Presentation of the Findings

The findings from data analysis presented pertain to responses received from surveys of a small group of government contracting employees from an organization in the mid-Atlantic region. Eight government contracting employees answered 8 survey questions. To protect participants' privacy, I replaced participants' names with codes such as E1, E2, through E8. Based on the survey questions, participants presented responses that varied in range and complexity. As previously noted, using the techniques employed under Dibley's assessment of McCormack's lenses, I represented each participant's experience in an unbiased manner. Some employees' findings were in line with those of some managers; however, differences were considered and noted. Various themes emerged which show parallels and variances among employees. Findings are based results of data analysis of the survey questions.

5.3.1 Issues Employees Face Regarding Unethical Behaviors.

In regard to issues government contracting employees face regarding unethical behaviors when doing their jobs, 50% of participants noted no issues while 25% assessed conflicting policies as a cause of their inability to do the job ethically (see Table 6). P6 and P8 posited that the organization stresses warfighter needs as paramount; therefore, employees feel that there is little choice in offering contracts to vendors, whether or not the price offered by the vendor is reasonable. Participants noted that sometimes working with a specific vendor is easier than assigning a contract by competition. If an employee is forced to offer contracts to specific vendors instead of offering competitive advantage to all eligible businesses, that employee may become complacent and therefore more vulnerable to a vendor offering bribes for government contract/awards.

Table 6 *Nodes Related to Frequency of Themes for Issues Employees Face Regarding Unethical Behaviors*

Theme	*n*	% of frequency of occurrence
None	4	50%
Fear of reprisal	1	10%
Conflicting policies	2	25%
Fear of failure	1	10%

Note: n=frequency

Urgency of need can outweigh ethical contracting. These findings contradict managers' assessments and organizational policies that stressed ethical requirements as a must when doing government contracting business. Although the percentage of employees who noted issues that could cause unethical behaviors is large, we must keep in mind that the statistics are based on a small group of employees.

5.3.2 Fundamentals Used to Perform Duties Ethically.

Participants' assessed that fundamentals used in helping them to do their jobs ethically included government contracting regulations such as the FAR and DFARS as well as local regulations (see Table 7). Sixty-three percent of participants posited that the FAR and DFARS were the primary guidance used. When asked what management's role was in helping employees to understand the ethical requirements listed in the regulations, employees attested that managers were *hands-off.* For example, E-6 stated that without personal ethical values it would be easy to do the *wrong* thing. E3 noted that managers provide the regulations but are rarely available to assist employees in understanding the regulations.

Table 7 *Nodes Related to Theme - Fundamentals Used to Perform Duties Ethically*

Theme	n	% of frequency of occurrence
FAR, DFARS	5	63%
Local Guidance	3	38%

Note: n=frequency

Employees contradict managers' assessment of being involved in ensuring employees understand ethical requirements of government contracting. These government contracting employees affirm the previous assessment that managers must guide their employees and not just lead them. Employees not offered ethical guidance and who do not possess the moral fiber to be ethical can easily be influenced to be unethical.

Understanding government contracting overall ethical philosophy will move government contracting employees to do their jobs to the letter of the law.

5.3.3 Elements of Organizational Philosophy that Employees Use to do Ethical Contracting.

Thirty-eight percent of participants assessed that no specific element is used to implement the government contracting ethical requirements (see Table 8). The same employees posited that no specific element was used because the organizational philosophies were unclear. Twenty-five percent of participants noted clarity in understanding the organizations ethical requirements. E-1 stated that their manager ensured that the organization's ethical policies were explained and understood. Participants posited that government contracting managers stressed *the bottom-line* and show little regard to how employees accomplish it. Some participants showed frustration with the ethical requirement process.

Table 8 *Nodes Related to Theme - Elements of Organizational Philosophy Employees Use*

Theme	n	% of frequency of occurrence
Clearly understanding Policy	2	25%
Objectivity, confidentiality, professionalism	1	13%
Integrity, morals	2	25%
No specific element used	3	38%
Document and report improprieties	1	13%

Note: n=frequency

Twenty-five percent of participants posited that personal morals and integrity guide their ethical climate. Participants agreed with previous researchers that morally, the burden of making decisions between normal expectations and personal ethics can prove daunting. E-3 noted that individuals are responsible for their actions. However, if employees are not shown or taught ethical requirements and the consequences of going outside the scope of those requirements, they may make decisions contrary to the government's ethical requirements. If employees are provided clear understanding of government contracting ethical policies, employees' ethical personas may come through in the end.

5.3.4 Integrity

Integrity is important in building a relationship with customers as well as establishing social responsibility. An organization whose leadership shows lack of ethics and integrity stands the chance of losing customers, and therefore, losing dollars. The organization that conducts itself ethically whether or not it is under public or legal scrutiny is an organization that portrays good business ethics and social responsibility. How employees in an organization conduct themselves can have a direct impact on society;[12] the employees' behaviors are based on the concept of corporate social responsibility.[102]

Corporate social responsibility is organizational leadership posing regulations on the organization's members which keep the organization compliant with the laws and ethical standards as set forth by society (i.e. consumers, stakeholders, and public sphere).[102] In order for organizations to gain and maintain societal trust, members of the organization must show good judgment. Organizational leadership must emphasize ethical standards, merit, and honesty to their employees and the employees must portray integrity to organizational leadership and society.

Employees may feel that they have no avenue in which to turn if unethical issues occur and managers pull back from assisting employees, citing regulations, and sometimes leaving the employees feeling helpless. Organizational management who are not actively involved in employees training in ethical practices leaves each U.S. federal government contracting employee with a sense of hopelessness.[35] Some U.S. federal government contracting employees may feel they have no viable resources in which to turn. U.S. federal government contracting employees may be motivated to conduct themselves ethically if they receive training and guidance in regards to contracting ethical requirements.

5.3.5 Culture, Beliefs, and Trust

Individuals are capable of ethical integrity.[142] The individual's environment, culture, organizational structure, and individual beliefs all combine to enforce ethical integrity. Ethical business culture goes hand-in-hand with leadership and ethical climate.[4] The business culture and ethical climate of an organization's leadership may influence how ethical an employee might be and contributes to productivity in the workplace. Culture is based on combinations of individual and organizational leadership's behaviors, attitudes, and beliefs. The organizational and/or individual's working environment may play a role in the way that culture, belief, and trust are incorporated into daily working activities.

The employee's culture and beliefs may influence their ethical behavior. Corporate culture assists organizational leadership in maintaining the values of the organization; if the organizational culture is positive, employees may portray positive values.[4] Organizational culture and beliefs can also play a significant role in employee conduct. Employees who feel that their input makes a difference will be more apt to protect the organization than employees who feels they are just in the organization to do a job.[183]

5.3.6 Ethical Practices

Employees' ethical behavior is essential to socially responsible business practices. Ethics in the U.S. federal government contracting is a public trust.[43] The study of ethics in the U.S. federal government contracting is significant because ethics has a major role in ensuring that a U.S. federal government contracting organization is successful.[47] U.S. federal government organizations can utilize whistle-blowing and/or internal reporting to encourage employees to report any ethical violations that they may witness.[202] If employees are encouraged to report what they see, they are more likely to act ethically.[107] Organizations should provide a forum in which employees can feel free to discuss ethical issues without fear of reprisal; training should also be readily available that includes the parameters of ethics, organizational morals and values, and employer/employee expectations concerning ethical conduct.[12] If employees understand what ethics are, and are given adequate training, they should have the tools required to discern right or wrong behavior.[138]

5.3.7 Challenges Employees Face in Ethically Implementing Organization Philosophy.

Participants noted challenges confronted in determining implementation of government contracting ethical philosophies. Challenges noted include included (a) contradictory policies and procedures, (b) changing environment, (c) conflict between government contracting policies and customer needs, and (d) determining ethical implementation of the policies. Participants posited that contradictory policies and lack of consistency proves challenging when attempting to implement government contracting ethical requirements (see Table 9). E-6 noted that at times local organization policies appear conflicting in regards to government contracting policies. Participants stated that local policies stress *customer first and always* while government contracting policies stress customer service and ethical government contracting.

Table 9 *Nodes Related to Theme - Challenges Employees Face*

Theme	*n*	% of frequency of occurrence
Contradictory policies	4	50%
Lack of consistency	3	38%
Changing environment	3	38%
Determining ethical implementation of policy	1	13%

Note: n=frequency

Participants assessed that managers push employees to *buy-buy-buy* without regard to the challenges employees face in purchasing goods and services at fair and reasonable prices. Participants posited that challenges employees face make it easy to accept bribes from particular vendors for unwarranted contracts. Participants discount the assessment that customer service and customer satisfaction encompass the administration of government contracts. Although matching organization and customer values can produce a customer-centric environment; participants assessed that putting customer needs before organizational ethical requirements can produce a lackadaisical environment.

5.3.8 Training/Development Methods Used. How Can Methods be Improved?

In regards to training or development methods managers used to guide government contracting employees to administer contracts ethically, 38% of participants noted local organizational training as primary to employees' development and understanding of government contracting ethical requirements while 63% assessed that mandatory training was key (see Table 10). Local training is not necessarily mandatory and vice versa. Mandatory training is not always administered locally. For example, organizations may provide training such as employee development classes that is suggested but not mandatory for employees to attend. On the other hand, mandatory training such as those required for certifications [i.e. *The* Defense Acquisition Workforce Improvement Act *(DAWIA)* certification classes] are not always offered locally. As noted by 5 participants, mandatory training plays a vital role in ensuring that any changes in organizational policies are clearly outlined. As previously stated, findings from this study enforce the assessment that incorporating into the training government contracting requirements, compliance with the law, and customer satisfaction encourages ethical behaviors.[193]

Participants posited that management's providing training on the fundamentals of the FAR, DFARS, and local ethical guidance might present further opportunities for employees to understand the requirements of doing their jobs ethically. As noted, formal ethics training encourages ethical organizational development; therefore, it may decrease instances of unethical behaviors.[231] Thirteen percent of participants believed that listening to and accepting employees' input on their training requirements might be beneficial. Participants attest that unless managers have open dialogue with employees they will not understand what employees know, understand, or need.

Table 10 *Nodes Related to Theme - Training/Development Methods Used.*

Theme	*n*	% of frequency of occurrence
Mandatory training courses	5	63%
Local training	3	38%
Listen and accept employees' input	1	13%
Not enough relevant training offered	2	25%
Offer training based on survey results	1	13%
Provide peer-to-peer, mentor-to-mentee, etc	2	25%
Training is sufficient	3	38%

Note: n=frequency

Employees agree that different managers have different styles, views, and ideas. Participants noted that government contracting leaders distribute surveys to assess government contracting climate; however, suggestions made in the surveys are not always implemented. Participants posited that uniformity is needed across all spectrum of government contracting. Relying on policies and guidance such as the FAR, DFARS, and local policies to guide employees to do their jobs ethically is good; however, if each manager interprets policies differently employees may be confused as to which standards they should follow.

Thirteen percent of participants suggested having comprehensive peer-to-peer or mentoring training (see Table 10). Participants affirmed that positive mentoring is vital to government contracting employees' ethical implementation of government contracts. Managers have the responsibility to ensure that employees in their charge are motivated in the right direction. Communicating with employees might offer managers opportunities to detect potential problems they might not notice if employees were left to their own devices

5.3.9 Benefits of Ethical Government Contracting.

Participants stressed the benefits of mitigating government contracting employees' unethical behaviors. Benefits included (a) cost savings, (b) better use of taxpayer dollars, (c) improvements to customer service, (d) self-satisfaction, (e) improvement in workforce performance and (f) less frustration in doing their jobs. Seventy-five percent of participants stressed cost savings to the government, customer, and taxpayer as the primary benefit of ethical government contracting (see Table 11). E1, E5, and E8 posited that spending taxpayer dollars wisely improves society's views of government contracting organizations.

Table 11 *Nodes Related to Theme - Benefits of Ethical Government Contracting*

Theme	*n*	% of frequency of occurrence
Cost savings, better use of taxpayer dollars	6	75%
Improved customer service	2	25%
Self-satisfaction, confidence	3	38%
Improved workforce	1	13%
Less frustration with doing the job	1	13%

Note: n=frequency

Employees noted self-satisfaction as an added benefit of ethical government contracting. As noted in Table 11, 38% of participants posited that self-satisfaction and self-confidence were beneficial to doing their jobs ethically. E-7 posited that doing the job well provides a feeling of self-gratification and delight in doing the job based on personal morals and government contracting ethical policies. Participants' views on the benefits of employees doing their jobs ethically affirm managers' and organizational guidance that saving money and doing the job ethically benefits all stakeholders as well as society.

Results from this study confirm previous findings that focusing on the broader area of stakeholder management and social responsibility enhances ethical compliance within government contracting. Thirteen percent of participants noted reduced frustration in doing their job (see table 11). E4 posited that doing the job ethically benefits all stakeholders and improves the government contracting workforce. As noted within the conceptual framework of this study, changes to government contracting policies can benefit all stakeholders. Incorporating ethics into organizational strategies benefits not only the organization but also all stakeholders[67]. Benefiting stakeholders includes good customer service.

6

APPLICATION TO PROFESSIONAL PRACTICE AND IMPLICATIONS FOR CHANGE

Professionalism is the skill, good judgement, and polite behavior expected from an individual who is trained to do a job well. – Merriam-Webster

6.1 Introduction to Professional Practice – What Changes are Needed?

As previously assessed, government contracting employees' unethical behaviors create an impression of widespread ethical violations in government contracting organizations.[44] Taxpayers lose billions of dollars annually to public procurement fraud. Managers should assist their employees in eliminating unethical behaviors; however, researchers noted the inability of managers to adapt best business practices that combine regulations and responsibility.[46] Managers can influence their employees both positively and negatively. Government contracting managers must strive to be positive role models.

This section contains the results of analysis of the above-mentioned study. In addition, Section 3 contains an overview of the study, the findings of the study, and applications for professional practice. I reviewed (a) implications for social change, (b) recommendations for action, including dissemination of results, (c) recommendation for further study on government contracting managers' perceived level of understanding of government contracting ethical regulations, (d) reflections of my experience conducting this research study, as well as (e) the study summary and conclusions.

6.2 Applications to Professional Practice

In FY2012, the President's Budget Request included $204 billion for acquisitions. The size of the budget used with government contracting organizations offers more opportunities for unethical behaviors by government contracting employees. The U.S. government took steps to deter government contracting employees' unethical behaviors by making changes to the FAR that specify requirements for ethical conduct and punishments for non-compliance. Although government contracting administrators made changes to the FAR designed to reduce unethical behaviors, no academic literature is available that shows if the changes had desired effects.

The findings from this study indicated a vital need for additional government contracting managers' training and guidance in mitigating unethical behaviors by employees administering government contracts. The threat of increased unethical behaviors by government contracting employees, coupled with the stated need for simplification and clarification of government contracting regulations, support the conclusion that vagueness in procurement policies can affect all stakeholders.[40] The findings relate to stakeholder theory because as identified by D1 in the second theme, government contracting organizations can establish trust through engagement with all stakeholders.

Moral principles must drive stakeholder relations.[55] Government contracting managers must guide their employees in understanding how unethical behaviors affect not only the organization but also all stakeholders. The ethical principles of government contracting business as defined in the FAR as well as outlined in D1 can provide government contracting organizations with better performance approaches if managers know how to manage employees. The ability of managers to reduce employees' unethical behaviors will benefit not only this organization but also all stakeholders.

To some extent, the findings of this study suggest that unethical behaviors by government contracting employees may be consistent with lack of information provided by their managers. If the managers do not have clear guidance and training in understanding ethical requirements, they cannot provide that information to employees.[105] On the other hand, if policies, regulations, and guidance are unclear, managers will provide varied personal interpretations to individual employees. There must be clarity and consistency through the government contracting arena.

Implementing the views assessed in this study has important implications for government contracting because, as suggested by participants of this study, all stakeholders can benefit from ethical government contracting through improved customer service and increased cost savings. Improving customer service can show stakeholders and society improvement in the ethical culture of government contracting. Some participants suggested that reducing government contracting employees' unethical behaviors might stave off the effects of scandals currently plaguing government contracting organizations. When government contracting managers understand the requirements of ethical government contracting and know how to disseminate the information to their employees, employees may consider the consequences of their actions before making a decision to be unethical. The results of this study may assist organization leaders in developing strategies for improved implementation of ethical requirements.

6.3 Implications for Social Change

Positive social change is possible within government contracting. Society, policy administrators, government contracting professionals, and acquisition workforces must make an effort to clarify and simplify the ethical requirements of the government contracting process. From the data analysis, I concluded that a dominant association exists among understanding government contracting regulations, organizational philosophies, corporate best practices, and government contracting fraud. Furthermore, I concluded that the association that exists among these entities is vital to the government contracting community because of insights provided by the training attitudes, expectations, and transparency needed within government contracting.

Government contracting professionals may benefit from this study by understanding the potential effect of unethical behaviors on all stakeholders. Understanding the role that each stakeholder plays in the process, and how unethical behaviors can affect each member, may assist stakeholders in mitigating financial losses occurring yearly due to fraud, bribery, and abuse. In addition, this study may encourage socially accountable and transparent federal contracting processes that could reduce fraud, which in turn may renew society's trust in government contracting organizations.

Findings and conclusions from this study are expected to expand the scholarly literature that demonstrates the benefits of socially acceptable government contracting processes. Any reduction in government contracting employees' unethical behaviors can benefit society because individual taxpayers represent society. Government contracting organizations also benefit from increased ethical behaviors by employees by cost savings in reduction of prosecutions and lost production time. Businesses' leaders may benefit because the money saved by government contracting organizations can finance technology and innovations. Stakeholders can use money saved by government contracting organizations to incentivize human development, thereby benefiting society. Findings and recommendations from this study may contribute to positive social change by improving training and ethical standards, which could lead to enhancing society's trust in government contracting organizations.

6.4 Recommendations for Action

The findings indicated that some managers had the knowledge needed to assist employees in reducing unethical behaviors; however, changes to policies may still be needed. Findings from this study revealed dominant perceptions that there is a connection among (a) government contracting regulations, (b) government contracting manager and employee training, (c) trust, and (d) best business practices, to diminish the employees' unethical behaviors. Because of the findings, I propose three recommendations to both the government contracting officials/regulators and industry leaders.

First, I recommend that the government contracting officials/ regulators seek to improve dissemination of ethical guidelines on a regular basis, thereby improving government contracting managers and employees' understanding of the ethical guidelines. Stakeholders doing government contracting business require clarity. If the guidelines and regulations are unclear, government contracting employees may not fully comprehend the ramifications of continued unethical behaviors. Government contracting managers must drive ethical and value integration. Leaders have the power to motivate employees by being positive role models.[126]

My second recommendation is that government contracting officials conduct a more comprehensive review of instances of unethical behaviors by government contracting employees. One result of this review would be conducting *random checks* to ensure that employees are doing their jobs ethically; this may benefit all stakeholders. Managers must have the tools needed to assist their employees. Another result of this review might be to set up quarterly training on the FAR requirements in relation to ethical conduct. This can help both managers and employees to better to understand the ethical the requirements jobs. Along with FAR training, I recommend that managers receive quarterly ethical training. The training can include the requirements for ethical contracting, ethics in business, and the effect of unethical behaviors on the stakeholders. Government contracting managers must offer and maintain relevant training that provides government contracting employees with the tools needed to do the job ethically.

My third recommendation is that government contracting officials impose penalties that will reduce misconduct. The FAR lists penalties for government contracting employees' unethical behaviors. However, unless the individual takes the time to read FAR Part 3 inclusively, the possible ramifications of their unethical behaviors may not be clear. Mitigating depends on government contracting employees' believing that stakeholders might discover the acts of unethical behaviors and that the cost of the action is greater than the potential profit. I recommend that the government contracting administrators enable and empower managers to publish statistics of employees caught in unethical situations and the punishments for the employees' actions. Implementing these findings would support previous finding that corporate ethics programs educate and inform.

My fourth and final recommendation is that regulators update the current version of FAR Subpart 9.5 coverage on organizational conflicts of interest. Government contracting employees are not solely culpable in regards to taking bribes and behaving unethically. Companies who do business with government contracting organizations have a responsibility to also conduct themselves ethically. Offering profits to employees in exchange for lucrative contracts is both immoral and unethical. These company leaders should understand the ramifications of their actions. Updating the aforementioned guidance for a broad range of federal government contracting organizations might counter conflicts previously noted.

The research findings will benefit government contracting leaders who have a goal of positive social change within the government contracting system. After applying suggested changes, government contracting leaders can meet with government contracting managers to review both successes and failures regarding implementation. Government contracting managers must meet with employees to disseminate updated information and review lessons learned. There must be checks and balances to determine if applied changes made a difference.

6.5 Recommendations for Further Study

Findings from this study determined that government contracting managers have the desire to manage their employees ethically and assist employees in mitigating unethical behaviors; however, managers need clear policies, processes, and tools to accomplish those tasks. I recommend three studies to further the understanding of what managers need to reduce employees' unethical behavior. First, I recommend a comparative study to discover if changes to FAR Part 3 have reduced the number of reported instances of unethical behaviors. The results of such a study might further the understanding of what is needed to alleviate unethical behaviors in government contracting.

Next, I recommend further study of a broader base of government contracting managers to determine the level of understanding of government contracting ethical regulations. Within this study, researchers could address three issues: (a) government contracting managers' knowledge of the FAR, (b) the likelihood of government contracting managers' detecting unethical behaviors in their employees, and (c) if managers can articulate the aspects of *deterrence theory* based on previous assessment that punishment for violations will surpass reward.

Finally, I recommend further evaluation of government contracting managers' understanding of what each manager needs to assist their employees' in mitigating possible unethical behaviors. Researchers may expand on the current study by perusing a broader spectrum of government contracting managers based on multiple organizations and employees managed. Findings from the envisioned research studies may enhance the understanding of both academia and government contracting stakeholders on the association of (a) government contracting managers' understanding, (b) government contracting employees' ethical conduct, and (c) society's need for clarity in government contracting. The expectation is that findings from this study may lead to enhanced future research focused on clarification of government contracting regulations, enhanced training for government contracting employees and managers, and reduction in unethical behaviors within government contracting arenas.

6.6 Reflections

Interviewing participants to gain an understanding of the requirements that the government contracting managers needed to lessen unethical behaviors by employees was both fascinating and informative. Learning the history of government contracting, discovering various instances of unethical behaviors by employees, and seeing the government contracting leaders' efforts to combat unethical behaviors heightened my understanding of the subject. With more than 25 years of experience in government contracting, I had preconceived ideas of what to expect prior to conducting this study. I initiated this study with the preconceived notion that all personnel understood the ethical requirements of government contracting and that managers had all the tools needed to supervise their employees. Over time, I learned to bracket my biases and maintain an objective, scholarly, and unbiased approach to my research. The change in attitude proved invaluable in the research process and more importantly, in gaining an understanding of the difficulties that each government contracting manager faces.

Completing the dissertation process taught me the value of applying structured and unbiased approaches to problems and challenges. The frustrations experienced during the dissertation process, from re-writes to waiting for approvals, taught me that anything worth doing is worth the time, hard work, and patience that I was required to bring to bear. I became open to exploring literature on topics not previously considered; I learned to master patience and listen instead of thinking that I knew what the answer would be; and I learned to analyze data objectively. My focus changed from an attitude of knowing, to listening and understanding. My lived experiences informed my point of view that government contracting managers are individuals who need the same guidance as their employees. Overall, completing this study significantly expanded my knowledge concerning government contracting regulations and ethical requirements, and most importantly, my awareness of government contracting managers' needs regarding the need for an ethical contracting knowledge base. The knowledge gained, and ideas expressed by government contracting managers significantly contributed to this study.

Summary and Conclusions

This study gave me an overview of government contracting managers' understanding of the requirements needed to mitigate government contracting employees' unethical behaviors. The research methodology followed a qualitative case study that included a purposeful sampling of 21 government contracting managers. The data collection process included semistructured interviews and documentation as research techniques. My findings showed that most government contracting managers had not experienced employee unethical behaviors; however, those managers who offered an opinion provided specific examples of issues that government contracting managers face in mitigating employees' unethical behaviors. Most of the participants understood the mandate to incorporate codes of ethics into government contracting. Based on established guidelines, participants articulated that ethics are mandatory when doing government contracting business. Ethical behavior should be guided by universal principles and moral values. Moreover, government contracting organizational standards is influenced by core values of honesty and integrity; managers' interpretation of those principles determines implementation of the standards.

Section 1 of this study included a variety of topics and strategies such as the problem and purpose of the research. I assessed the nature of the study, identifying and describing the research question, looking at the conceptual framework, and the literature review of the study. Previous sections of this paper mentioned major previous works and their main findings. In Section 2, the focus was the project. I built on the foundation given in Section 1, with the research method and design used to assess elements of the managerial knowledge needed to prevent government contracting employees' unethical behaviors. In section 3, I will explain and documented the findings of the study, addressing implications for social change and presenting explanations for actions deemed necessary for further study of this research topic. I will conclude with reflections on the research process.

The objective in Section 3 of this research was to assess the purpose of the research, examine the role of the researcher and analyze the selection of individuals participating in the research study. I looked at the data collection process and provided an explanation of reliability and validity methods. I detailed the findings of the research and explained applications of professional practices, implications for social change, and recommendations for future research study in Section 3.

Findings of this study show a desire of managers to assist their employees' in eliminating unethical behaviors. Deterring unethical behaviors benefit all stakeholders. A multi-dimensional approach to ethical government contracting starts with the government contracting managers. This study is a starting point to assisting government contracting organizations in providing the tools needed by their managers to build and reinforce ethical contracting values. Finally, this study showed the government contracting managers' desire to cultivate positive benefits to the organization, society, and employees; however, the task of mitigating government contracting employees' unethical behavior remains.

APPENDIX (1): GLOSSARY OF TERMS

Acquisition procedures prescribed in relevant subsections of the Federal Acquisition Regulation (FAR) relate to the purchase of goods and services. As used herein, the term "acquisition" generally applies to process, procedures, and services related to federal government contracting.

Agency is any entity of the Department of Defense (DoD) Component as follows: Department of the Army; Department of the Navy; Department of the Air Force; Defense Commissary Agency; Defense Contract Audit Agency; Defense Finance and Accounting Service; Defense Intelligence Agency; Defense Investigative Security Service; Defense Logistics Agency; Defense Mapping National Geospatial-Intelligence Agency; Defense Nuclear Threat Reduction Agency; Defense Information Systems Agency; National Security Agency; Office of the Inspector General of the Department of Defense (IG, DoD); and the Uniformed Services University of the Health Sciences. Employees of DoD Components not designated as separate Agencies, including employees of the Office of the Secretary of Defense (OSD), shall be treated as employees of DoD which shall be treated as a separate Agency.

Bribery is manipulating an action for personal gain by offering goods or services to an individual doing official government duties.

Communication – the process of using words, sounds, or behaviors to exchange information or express ideas, thoughts, or feelings to someone else. – Merriam-Webster

Conflict of interest in government contracting applies when government contracting employee presents dissonance when he/she does not provide impartial service when administering a contract.

A *Contract* is an agreement that specifies business transactions between qualified private organizations and the government.

Contracting Ethics is the continuation of the integrity of government contracting and assuring fair treatment to all approved government suppliers/contractors when administering government contracts.

Contractor/Supplier is an individual, firm, corporation, partnership, association, or other legal non-Federal entity that enters into a contract directly with government contracting component to furnish services, supplies, or both, including construction.

Core competency provides that an organization excels in a specified area of business and contributes sustainability to maintain a competitive advantage.[190]

Corporate governance is based on rules and regulations that regulate the rights and responsibilities of stakeholders by controlling all aspects of the organization.

Corporate reputation: Corporate reputation represents the external stakeholders' views and classifications of a firm's past and future performance.[159]

Defense Competition provides that competition is the ability of an organization to improve performance while reducing cost.

Federal Acquisition Regulations (FAR) outlines procurement policies and procedures used in government contracting.

Federal Government Outsourcing. Government contracting organizations outsource services previously performed by government agencies to private companies for the purpose of efficiency, cost cutting, politics, and competition.

Federal regulations: Federal regulations represent the rules implemented to encourage ethical actions during an economic transaction.[99]

Fraud: Fraud represents an action conducted that illegally takes property from others.[144]

Government contracting requires government contracting organizations to obtain goods and services from private companies. Government contracting includes identification of goods and service, source selection, contract award, and contract administration.

Government contracting employees are business leaders working for the benefit of government entities, customers, and community. The FAR authorizes government contracting employees to enter into, administer, or terminate contracts.

Gratuity as defined in 5 C.F.R. 2635.203(b) is acceptance of gifts, favors, entertainment, loans, or anything of monetary value in exchange for favors from contracts. Subpart 3.1 of the FAR clarifies standards of conduct, policies, and procedures for avoiding personal conflicts of interest.

The Small Business Administration (SBA) defines *Historically Underutilized Business Zones (HUBZone)* as a program that helps small businesses in urban and rural communities to gain preferential access to federal procurement opportunities.

Integrity refers to adherence to moral or ethical principles; honesty. – Dictionary.com

Opportunism is pursuing a person's self-interest by way of deceit and betrayal.[109]

Procurement as used in this publication is related to the act of buying goods and services for federal government contracting agencies and customers.

Regulations: Regulations are guidelines created to restrict ethical behaviors and activities.[181]

Reputation: Reputation is the public's concerns that develops over time primarily on the emotional, economic, societal, and traditional connection between an organization and its stakeholders.[25]

Small Disadvantaged Businesses (SDB) are those organizations that meet specific criteria defined by the SBA. Criteria include having 51% or more of the business owned and controlled by one or more disadvantaged person, the company must be small according to the SBA's size standards, and the disadvantaged individual(s) must be socially or economically disadvantaged.

Social Change includes changes in social institutions, social behaviors, and social relations with individuals and organizations.

Socioeconomic relates to combinations of social and economic factors that may but an organization at a disadvantage to do business with government contracting organizations.

Tolerance as defined by Merriam-Webster is the willingness to endure opinions or behaviors that one does not agree with.

Trust is the desire to take a chance to the extent of having clear objectives and assurance in the words and actions of others.

APPENDIX (2): ABBREVIATED TERMS

ARRA - American Recovery and Reinvestment Act
ASPA - American Society for Public Administration
C.F.R. - Code of Federal Regulations
CICA - Competition in Contracting Act
DAWIA - Defense Acquisition Workforce Improvement Act
DFARS - Defense Acquisition Regulations Supplement
DoD - Department of Defense
DOJ - Department of Justice
ESRS - Electronic Subcontracting Reporting System
FAR - Federal Acquisition Regulation
FARA - Federal Acquisition Reform Act
FASA - Federal Acquisition Streamlining Act
FBI - Federal Bureau of Investigations
FPASA - Federal Property and Administrative Services Act
FPDS - Federal Procurement Data Systems
GAO - Government Accountability Office
GS – General Schedule
GSAM - General Service Administration Manual
IRB – Institutional Review Board
MED - Microenterprise Development Programs
NIH - National Institutes of Health
OIG - Office of the Inspector General
OGE - Office of Government Ethics
OMB – Office of Management and Budget
OPM - Office of Personnel Management

SAM - System for Award Management
SBA - Small Business Administration
SDB - Small-Disadvantage Business
SME - Subject Matter Experts
SOP - Standard operating procedures
SOX - Sarbanes-Oxley Act
U.S.C. – United States Code

APPENDIX (3): REFERENCES

[1]   Adams, G. B., & Balfour, D. L. (2010). Market-based government and the decline of organizational ethics. *Administration and Society, 42*, 615-637. doi:10.1177/0095399710381347

[2]   Ailon, G. (2012). The discursive management of financial risk scandals: The case of Wall Street Journal commentaries on LTCM and Enron. *Qualitative Sociology, 35*, 251-270. doi:10.1007/s11133-012-9217-5

[3]   Amey, S. H. (2012). The importance of contract design. *Public Administration Review, 72*, 697-698. doi:10.111/j-1540-6210.2012.02624.x

[4]   Ardichvili, A., & Jondle, D. (2009). Ethical Business Cultures: A Literature Review and Implications for HRD. *Human Resource Development Review,* 8(2), 223-244.

[5]   Awortwi, N. (2012). Contracting out local government services to private agents: An analysis of contract design and service delivery performance in Ghana. *International Journal of Public Administration, 35*, 886-900. doi:10. 1080/01900692.2012.686033

[6]   Ayuso, S., Rodriguez, M. A., Garcia-Castro, R., & Arino, M. A. (2012). Maximizing stakeholders' interests: An empirical analysis of the stakeholder approach to corporate governance. *Business & Society, 51*(3), 1-26. doi:10.1177/0007650311433122

[7]   Azim, M. I. (2012). Corporate governance mechanisms and their impact on company performance: A structural equation model analysis. *Australian Journal of Management, 37*, 481-505. doi:10.1177/0312896212451032

[8]   Baker, S. D., & Comer, D. R. (2012). "Business ethics everywhere": An experimental exercise to develop students' ability to identify and respond to ethical issues in business. *Journal of Management Education, 32*, 95-125. doi:10.1177/1052562911408071

[9] Bansal, P., & Corley, K. (2011). The coming of age for qualitative research: Embracing the diversity of qualitative methods. *Academy of Management Journal, 54*, 233-237. doi:10.5465/AMJ.2011.60262792

[10] Bansal, P., & DesJardine, M. R. (2014). Business sustainability: It is about time. *Strategic Organization, 12*, 70-78. doi:10.1177/1476127013520265

[11] Bao, G., Wang, X., Larsen, G. L., & Morgan, D. F. (2013). Beyond new public governance a value-based global framework for performance management, governance, and leadership. *Administration & Society, 45*, 443-467. doi:10.1177/0095399712464952

[12] Batten, J. A., George, R. J., & Hettihewa, S. (2007). Is Corporate Ethical Practice Changing? Evidence from Sri-Lanka. *Asia Pacific Business Review, 13*(1), 59-78. doi:10.1080/13602380601010532

[13] Beeri, I., Dayan, R., & Vigoda-Gadot, E. (2013). Advancing ethics in public organizations: The impact of an ethics program on employees' perceptions and behaviors in a regional council. *Journal of Business Ethics, 112*, 59-78. doi:10.1007/s10551-012-1232-7

[14] Bergman, J. Z., Rentsch, J. R., Small, E. E., Davenport, S. W., & Bergman, S. M. (2012). The shared leadership process in decision-making teams. *The Journal of Social Psychology, 152*, 17-42. doi:10.1080/00224545.2010.538763

[15] Biddle, R. E., & Biddle, D. A. (2013) What public-sector employees need to know about promotional practices, procedures, and tests in public safety promotional processes: After Ricci v. DeStefano. *Public Personnel Management, 42*, 151-190. doi:10.1177/0091026013487046

[16] Bota-Avram, C. (2013). Is ethical behavior of companies influenced by governance? *International Advances in Economic Research, 19*, 325-326. doi:10.1007/s11294-013-9427-y

[17] Bradbury, M. D. (2011). Ledbetter v. Goodyear: Circumscribing Title VII's discrimination protections. *Public Personnel Management, 40*, 185-192. doi:10.1177/009102601104000301

[18] Bradshaw, J., & Chang, S. (2013). Past performance as an indicator of future performance: Selecting an industry partner to maximize the probability of program success. *Defense Acquisition Research Journal, 20*(1), 49-70. Retrieved from hhtp://www.dau.mil

[19] Bromberg, D. (2014). Can vendors buy influence? The relationship between campaign contributions and government contracts. *International Journal of Public Administration, 37*, 556-567. doi:10.1080/01900692.2013.879724

[20] Brown, E. (2013). Vulnerability and the basis of business ethics: From fiduciary duties to professionalism. *Journal of Business Ethics, 113*, 489-504. doi:10.1007/s10551-012-1318-2

[21] Bumgarner, J., & Newswander, C. B. (2012). Governing alone and with partners: Presidential governance in a post-NPM environment. *Administration & Society, 44*, 546-570. doi:10.1177/0095399711413869

[22] Campbell, J. L., Quincy, C., Osserman, J., & Pedersen, O. K. (2013). Coding in-depth semistructured interviews: Problems of unitization and intercoder reliability and agreement. *Sociological Methods & Research, 42*, 294-320. doi:10.1177/0049124113500475

[23] Carroll, A. B. (1979). A three-dimensional conceptual model of corporate performance. *Academy of Management Review, 4*, 497-505. doi:10.5465/AMR.1979.4498296

[24] Cassematis, P., & Wortley, R. (2013). Prediction of Whistleblowing or Non-reporting Observation: The Role of Personal and Situational Factors. *Journal Of Business Ethics, 117*(3), 615-634. doi:10.1007/s10551-012-1548-3

[25] Chanson, G., & Quelin, B. V. (2013). Decentralization and contracting out: A new pattern for internal and external barriers of the firm. *European Management Journal, 31*, 602-612. doi:10.1016/j.emj.2013.02.002

[26] Chevallier, C., Molesworth, C., & Happé, F. (2012). Diminished social motivation negatively impacts reputation management: Autism spectrum disorders as a case in point. *Plos ONE, 7*(1), 1-6. doi:10.1371/journal.pone.0031107

[27] Clark, K. (2011). Ethics, employees, and contractors: Financial conflicts of interest in and out of government. *Alabama Law Review, 62*(5), 961-1004. Retrieved from http://www.law.ua.edu.lawreview

[28] Coenen, M., Stamm, T., Stucki, G., & Cieza, A. (2012). Individual interviews and focus groups in patients with rheumatoid arthritis: A comparison of two qualitative methods. *Quality of Life Research, 21*, 359-370. doi:10.1007/s11136-011-9943-2

[29] Cohn, L. P. (2011). It wasn't in my contract: Security privatization and civilian control. *Armed Forces and Society, 37*, 381-398. doi:10.1177/0095327X10388135

[30] Collins, S. M. (2011). Diversity in the post affirmative action labor market: A proxy for racial progress? *Critical Sociology, 37*, 521-540. doi:10.1177/0896920510380075

[31] Costantino, N., Dotoli, M., Falagario, M., & Sciancalepore, F. (2012). Balancing the additional costs of purchasing and the vendor set dimension to reduce public procurement costs. *Journal of Purchasing and Supply Management, 18*, 189-198. doi:10.1016/j.pursup.2012.08.001

[32] Covell, C. L., Sidani, S., & Ritchie, J. A. (2012). Does the sequence of data collection influence participants' responses to closed and open-ended

questions? A methodological study. *International Journal of Nursing Studies, 49*, 664-671. doi:10.1016/j.ijnurstu.2011.12.002

[33] Cox, T. M. (2011). Is the Procurement Integrity Act "important" enough for the mandatory disclosure rule? A case for inclusion. *Public Contract Law Journal, 40*(2), 347-392. Retrieved from http://pclj.org

[34] Cribb, A. (2011). Integrity at work: Managing routine moral stress in professional roles. *Nursing Philosophy, 12*, 119-127. doi:10.111/j.1466-769X.2011.00484.x

[35] Currie, G., & Lockett, A. (2007). A critique of transformational leadership: moral, professional and contingent dimensions of leadership within public services organizations. *Human Relations*, 60(2), 341-370.

[36] Curry, W.S. (2010). Transforming ethics in government contracting. *Contract Management, 50*(4), 48-56. Retrieved from http://www.ncmahq.org

[37] Damianakis, T., & Woodford, M. R. (2012). Qualitative research with small connected communities: Generating new knowledge while upholding research ethics. *Qualitative Health Research, 22*, 708-718. doi:10.1177/1049732311431444

[38] Datta, A., Jessup, L., Reed, R. (2011). Corporate reputation for commercialization of innovation: Does reputation match reality, and does innovation matter? *Technology & Investment, 2*(4), 256-272. Retrieved from http://www.scirp.org/Journal/Home.aspx?IssueID=1174

[39] Deegan, C. (2007). *Australian financial accounting* (3rd ed.). North Ryde, United Kingdom: McGraw-Hill.

[40] Demessie, D. (2012). A model of trade restrictiveness index: Its application and implications in public procurement. *Journal of Public Procurement, 12*(2), 189-220. Retrieved from http://www.pracademics.com/jopp

[41] Dennis, W. J. (2011). Entrepreneurship, small business and public policy levers. *Journal of Small Business Management, 49*, 149-162. doi:10.1111/j.1540-627X.2010.00316x

[42] Denzin, N. K. (2012). Triangulation 2.0. *Journal of Mixed Methods Research, 6*, 80-88. doi:10.1177/1558689812437186

[43] Dirks, K., & Skarlicki, D. (2009). The Relationship Between Being Perceived as Trustworthy by Coworkers and Individual Performance. *Journal of Management*, 35(1), 136-157.

[44] Djuraskovic, I., & Arthur, N. (2011). Heuristic inquiry: A personal journey of acculturation and identity reconstruction. *The Qualitative Report, 15*(6), 1569-1593. Retrieved from http://www.nova.edu

[45] Donaldson, T., & Preston, L. E. (1995). The stakeholder theory of corporation: Concepts, evidence and implications. *Academy of Management Review, 20* (1), 65-91. doi:10.5465/AMR.1995.9503271992

46   Draper, A., & Swift, J. A. (2011). Qualitative research in nutrition and dietetics: Data collection issues. *Journal of Human Nutrition and Dietetics, 24*, 3-12. doi:10.1111/j.1365-277X.2010.01117.x

47   Elango, B., Paul, K., Kundu, S.K., & Paudel, S.K. (2010). Organizational ethics, individual ethics, and ethical intentions in international decision-making. *Journal of Business Ethics 97*(4), 543-561. doi:10.1007/s10551-010-0524-z

48   Elcock, H. (2012). Ethics and the public interest: A question of morality. *Teaching Public Administration, 30*, 115-123. doi:10.1177/0144739412463221

49   Elmir, R., Schmied, V., Jackson, D., & Wilkes, L. (2011). Interviewing people about potentially sensitive topics. *Nurse Researcher, 19*(1), 12-16. Retrieved from http://nurseresearcher.rcnpublishing.co.uk

50   Elo, S., Kaariainen, M., Kanste, O., Polkki, T., Utriainen, K., & Kyngas, H. (2014). Qualitative content analysis: A focus on trustworthiness. *Sage Open, 4*, 1-10. doi:10.1177/2158244014522633

51   Eskerod, P., & Huemann, M. (2013). Sustainable development and project stakeholder management: What standards say. *International Journal of Managing Projects in Business, 6*, 36-50. doi:10.1108/17538371311291017

52   Finlay, L. (2012). Unfolding the phenomenological research process: Iterative stages of "seeing afresh". *Journal of Humanistic Psychology, 53*, 172-201. doi:10.1177/0022167812453877

53   Fisher, W. P. Jr., & Stenner, A. J. (2011). Integrating qualitative and quantitative research approaches via the phenomenological method. *International Journal of Multiple Research Approaches, 5*, 89-103. doi:10.5172/mra.2011.5.1.89

54   Flotts, M., & Diaz, P. A. (2012). Cognitive, cultural, and institutional capital: An approximation to a local development perspective. *International Social Work, 55*, 369-382. doi:10.1177/0020872812437225

55   Freeman, R. E. (1984). *Strategic management: A stakeholder approach.* Boston, MA: Pittman.

56   Fyke, J. P., & Buzzanell, P. M. (2013). The ethics of conscious capitalism: Wicked problems in leading change and changing leaders. *Human Relations, 66*, 1619-1643. doi:10.1177/0018726713485306

57   Gerring, J. (2011). How good is good enough? A multidimensional, best-possible standard for research design. *Political Research Quarterly, 64*, 625-636. doi:10.1177/1065912910361221

58   Gioia, D. A., Corley, K. G., & Hamilton, A. L. (2013). Seeking qualitative rigor inductive research notes on the Gioia methodology. *Organizational Research Methods, 16*, 15-31. doi:10.1177/1094428112452151

59   Goertz, G., & Mahoney, J. (2012). Methodological Rorschach tests: Contrasting interpretations in qualitative and quantitative research. *Comparative Political Studies, 46,* 236-251. doi:10.1177/0010414012466376

60   Gonzalez-Hermosillo, B., & Hesse, H. (2011). Global market conditions and systemic risk. *Journal of Emerging Market Finance, 10,* 227 - 252. doi:10.1177/097265271101000204

61   Greaney, A., Sheehy, A., Heffernan, C., Murphy, J., Mhaolrúnaigh, S. N., Heffernan, E., & Brown, G. (2012). Research ethics application: a guide for the novice researcher. *British Journal of Nursing, 21*(1), 38-43. Retrieved from http://www.markallengroup.com/ma-healthcare/

62   Griffith, J. A., Connelly, S., & Thiel, C. E. (2011). Leader deception influences on leader-member exchange and subordinate organizational commitment. *Journal of leadership and Organizational Studies, 18,* 508-521. doi:10.1177/1548051811403765

63   Gupta, A. D. (2012). Corporate social responsibility and strategy: A bird's eye view. *Global Business Review, 13,* 153-165. doi:10.1177/097215091101300110

64   Haahr, A., Norlyk, A., & Hall, E. O. (2014). Ethical challenges embedded in qualitative research interviews with close relatives. *Nursing Ethics, 2,* 6/15. doi:10.1177/0969733013486370

65   Halpern, B. H., & Snider, K. F. (2012). Products that kill and corporate social responsibility: The case of U.S. defense firms. *Armed Forces and Society, 38,* 604-624. doi:10.1177/0953227X11415490

66   Hardman, H. (2013). The validity of a grounded theory approach to research on democratization. *Qualitative Research, 13,* 635-649. doi:10.1177/1468794112445526

67   Harland, N., & Holey, E. (2011). Research and learning methodologies including open-ended questions in quantitative questionnaires-theory and practice. *International Journal of Therapy and Rehabilitation, 18*(9), 482-486. Retrieved from http://www.ijtr.co.uk/

68   Harris, J. D., Sapienza, H. J., & Bowie, N. E. (2009). Ethics and entrepreneurship. *Journal of Business Venturing, 24*(5), 407-418. doi: 10.1016/j.jbusvent.2009.06.001

69   Harrison, J. S., & Wicks, A. C. (2013). Stakeholder theory, value, and firm performance. *Business Ethics Quarterly, 23,* 97-124. doi:10.5840/beq20132314

70   Harvey, L. (2015). Beyond member checking: A dialogic approach to the research interview. *International Journal of Research & Method in Education, 38,* 23-38. doi:10.1080/1743727X.2014.914487

71   Hasnas, J. (2013). Whither stakeholders theory? A guide for perplexed revisited. *Journal of Business Ethics, 112,* 47-57. doi:10.1007/s10551-012-1231-8

72 Hayibor, S. (2012). Equity and expectancy considerations in stakeholder actions. *Business & Society, 51*, 220-262. doi:10.1177/0007650308323396

73 Hazzan, O., & Nutov, L. (2014). Teaching and learning qualitative research ≈ Conducting qualitative research. *Qualitative Report, 19*(24), 1-29. Retrieved from http://www.nova.edu/ssss/QR/index.html

74 Hibbert, P., Sillince, J., Diefenbach, T., & Cunliffe, A. L. (2014). Relationally reflexive practice: A generative approach to theory development in qualitative research. *Organizational Research Methods, 17*, 1-21. doi:10.1177/1094428114524829

75 Hoskins, M, L., & White, J. (2013). Relational inquiries and the research interview: Mentoring future researchers. *Qualitative Inquiry, 19*, 179-188. doi:10.1177/1077800412466224

76 Hossain, M., Mitra, S., Rezaee, Z., & Sarath, B. (2011). Corporate governance and earnings management in the pre – and post – Sarbanes-Oxley Act regimes: Evidence from implicated option backdating firms. *Journal of Accounting, Auditing and Finance, 26*, 279-315. doi:10.1177/0148558X11401218

77 Ivey, J. (2013). Interpretive phenomenology. *Pediatric Nursing, 39*(1), 27-27. Retrieved from http://www.pediatricnursing.net

78 Iwu-Egwuonwu, R. (2011). Corporate reputation & firm performance: Empirical literature evidence. *International Journal of Business and Management, 6*, 197-206. doi:10.5539/ijbm.v6n4p197

79 Jamnik, A. (2011). The challenges of business ethics-management and the question of ethics. *Tourism and Hospitality Management, 17*(1), 141-152. Retrieved from http://www.ssrn.com/en/

80 Jiahuan, L. (2013). How political are government contracting decisions? An examination of human service contracting determinants. *Public Administration Quarterly, 37*(2), 182-207. Retrieved from http://www.spaef.com/PAQ_PUB/index.html

81 Ji Young, C., & Eun-Hee, L. (2014). Reducing confusion about grounded theory and qualitative content analysis: Similarities and differences. *Qualitative Report, 19*(32), 1-20. Retrieved from http://www.nova.edu/ssss/QR/QR19/cho64.pdf

82 Jin, C., & Yeo, H. (2011). Satisfaction, corporate credibility, CEO reputation and leadership effects on public relationships. *Journal of Targeting, Measurement and Analysis for Marketing, 19*, 127-140. doi:10.1057/jt.2011.10

83 Jing, Y. (2012). From stewards to agents? Intergovernmental management of public-nonprofit partnerships in China. *Public Performance & Management Review, 36*, 230-252. doi:10.2753/PMR1530-9576360204

84 Johnson, T. R., Feng, P., Sitzabee, W., & Jernigan, M. (2013). Federal acquisition regulation applied alliancing contract practices. *Journal of*

Construction Engineering & Management, 139, 480-487. doi:10.1061(ASCE) CO.1943-7862.0000592

[85] Johnston, J. M., & Girth, A. M. (2012). Government contracts and "managing the market": Exploring the costs of strategic management responses to weak vendor competition. *Administration & Society, 44*, 3-29. doi:10.1177/0095399711417396

[86] Jorgensen, K. (2012). Players as coresearchers: Expert player perspective as an aid to understanding games. *Simulation & Gaming, 43*, 374-390. doi:10.1177/1046878111422739

[87] Jovanovic, G. (2011). Toward a social history of qualitative research. *History of Human Sciences, 24*, 1-27. doi:10.1177/0952695111399334

[88] Kaufman, A., & Englander, E. (2011). Behavioral economics, federalism, and the triumph of stakeholder theory. *Journal of Business Ethics, 102*, 421-438. doi:10.1007/s10551-011-0822-0

[89] Keeler, R. L. (2013). Managing outsourced administrative discretion. *State and Local Government Review, 45*, 183-188. doi:10.1177/0160323X13496108

[90] Kidalov, M. V., & Snider, K. F. (2011). US and European Public Procurement Policies for Small and Medium-Sized Enterprises (SME): A Comparative Perspective. *Business & Politics, 13*(4), 1-43. doi:10.2202/1469-3569.1367

[91] Kim, Y., & Brown, T. L. (2012). The importance of contract design. *Public Administration Review, 72*, 687-696. doi:10.1111/j.1540-6210.2012.02537

[92] Kisely, S., & Kendall, E. (2011). Critically appraising qualitative research: A guide for clinicians more familiar with quantitative techniques. *Australasian Psychiatry, 19*, 364-367. doi:10.3109/10398562.2011.562508

[93] Koch, L. C., Niesz, T., & McCarthy, H. (2014). Understanding and reporting qualitative research: An analytical review and recommendations for submitting authors. *Rehabilitation Counseling Bulletin, 57*, 131-143. doi:10.1177/0034355213502549

[94] Koenig, D. R. (2012). The governance of value(s). *Journal of Risk Management in Financial Institutions, 5*(2), 194-210. Retrieved from http://www.henrystewart.com

[95] Koro-Ljungberg, M., & Bussing, R. (2013). Methodological modifications in a longitudinal qualitative research design. *Field Methods, 25*, 423-440. doi:10.1177/1525822X12472877

[96] Kozlowski, S. W. J., Chao, G. T., Grand, J. A., Braun, M. T., & Kuljanin, G. (2013). Advancing multilevel research design: Capturing the dynamics of emergence. *Organizational Research Methods, 16*, 581-615. doi:10.1177/1094428113493119

97 Lai Fong, W., Azizan, N. A., & Samad, M. A. (2011). A strategic framework for value enhancing enterprise risk management. *Journal of Global Business & Economics, 2*(1), 23-47. Retrieved from http://www.globalresearch.com.my/

98 Lamothe, M., & Lamothe, S. (2012). What determines the formal versus relational nature of local government contracting. *Urban Affairs Review, 48*, 322-353. doi:10.1177/1078087411432418

99 Lamothe, S., & Lamothe, M. (2013). Understanding the differences between vendor types in local governance. *American Review of Public Administration, 43*, 709-728. doi:10.1177/027507401245437

100 Lansiti, M. (2012). Government IT procurement processes and free software. *Public Contract Law Journal, 41*(2), 197-232. Retrieved from http://www.abanet.org

101 Leonidou, L. C., Kvasova, O., Leonidou, C. N., & Chari, S. (2013). Business unethicality as an impediment to consumer trust: The moderating role of demographic and cultural characteristics. *Journal of Business Ethics, 112*, 397-415. doi:10.1007/s10551-012-1267-9

102 Lindgreen, A., & Swaen, V. (2010). Corporate social responsibility. *International Journal of Management Reviews, 12*(1), 1-7. doi:10.111 1/j.1468-2370.2009.00277

103 Loayza, N. V., & Servén, L. (2010). *Business regulation and economic performance* [Google Books]. doi:10.1596/978-0-8213-7407-8

104 Lohier, J. (2011). It's time for integrity in government contracting: Enforcing FAR Part 3 and FAR 52.219-14 against the business community. *Contract Management, 51*(1), 46-53. Retrieved from http://www.ncmahq.org

105 Lorne, F. T., & Dilling, P. (2012). Creating values for sustainability: Stakeholders engagement, incentive alignment, and value currency. *Economics Research International, 2012*, 1-9. doi:10.1155/2012/142910

106 Lumineau, F., Frechet, M., & Puthod, D. (2011). An organizational learning perspective on the contracting process. *Strategic Organization, 9*, 8-32. doi:10.1177/1476127011399182

107 MacNab, B., Brislin, R., Worthley, R., Galperin, B. L., Jenner, S., Lituchy, T. R., & ... Turcotte, M. (2007). Culture and Ethics Management. Whistle-blowing and Internal Reporting within a NAFTA Country Context. *International Journal of Cross Cultural Management, 7*(1), 5-28. doi:10.1177/1470595807075167

108 Malatesta, D., & Smith, C. R. (2012a). Balancing hazards in the design of local franchise contracts. *Urban Affairs Review, 48*, 615-641. doi:10.1177/1078087412440273

[109] Malatesta, D., & Smith, C. R. (2012b). Government contracts for legal services: Does a previous contracting relationship alter accountability? *State and Local Government Review, 44*, 113-126. doi:10.1177/0160323X12446617

[110] Manghani, K. (2011). Quality assurance: Importance of systems and standard operating procedures. *Perspectives in Clinical Research, 2*, 34-37. doi:10.4103/2229-3485.76288

[111] Marais, H, (2012). A multi-methodological framework for the design and evaluation of complex research projects and reports in business and management studies. *Electronic Journal of Business Research Methods, 10*(2), 64-76. Retrieved from http://www.academic-conferences.org/ejournals.htm

[112] Maser, S. M., Subbotin, V., & Thompson, F. (2010). *The bid-protest mechanism: Effectiveness and fairness in defense acquisitions?* Retrieved from http://www.williamette.edu

[113] Maser, S. M., & Thompson, F. (2013). Dispelling fear and loathing in government acquisition: A proposal for cultural governance in DoD source selections. *Journal of Public Procurement, 13*(3), 289-314. Retrieved from http://pracademics.com

[114] Maxwell, J. A. (2013). *Qualitative research design: An interactive approach* (3rd ed.). Thousand Oaks, CA: Sage.

[115] Mihai, B., & Alina, A. N. (2013). Business ethics implementation in the organizational culture of companies. *Annals of the University of Oradea, Economic Science Series, 22*(1), 44-53. Retrieved from http://steconomice. uoradea.ro/anale/en_index.html

[116] Mikecz, R. (2012). Interviewing elites: Addressing methodological issues. *Qualitative Inquiry, 18*, 482-493. doi:10.1177/1077800412442818

[117] Molina-Azorin, J. F. (2012). Mixed methods research in strategic management: Impact and applications. *Organizational Research Methods, 15*, 33-56. doi:10.1177/1094428110393023

[118] Mols, F. (2010). Harnessing market competition in PPP procurement: The importance of periodically taking a strategic view. *Australian Journal of Public Administration, 69*, 229-244. doi:10.1111/j.1467-8500.2010.00681

[119] Monahan, M., Shah, A., & Mattare, M. (2011). The road ahead: Micro enterprise perspectives on success and challenge factors. *Journal of Management Policy & Practice, 12*(4), 113-125. Retrieved from http://www. na-businesspress.com

[120] Morinder, G., Biguet, G., Mattsson, E., Marcus, C., & Larsson, U. (2011). Adolescents' perceptions of obesity treatment -- an interview study. *Disability and Rehabilitation, 33*, 999-1009. doi:10.3109/09638288.2010.520800

[121] Mothershed, A. A. (2012). The $435 hammer and $600 toilet seat scandals: Does media coverage of procurement scandals lead to procurement reform?

Public Contract Law Journal, 41(4), 855-880. Retrieved from http://www. abanet.org

[122] Mountain, A. (2011). A discussion of "through the looking glass". *Transactional Analysis Journal, 14*, 173-178. doi:10.1177/036215371104100214

[123] Mukhopadhyay, B. (2011). Evaluating public procurement. *Review of Market Integration, 3*, 21-68. doi:10.1177/097492211100300103

[124] Mukhopadhyay, S., & Gupta, R. K. (2014). Survey of qualitative research methodology in strategy research and implication for Indian researchers. *Vision: The Journal of Business Perspective, 18*, 109-123. doi:10.1177/0972262914528437

[125] Nackman, M. J., Rathbone, M. A., Myers, C. A., & Pannier, W. M. (2011). Aerospace and defense industries. *The International Lawyer, 45*(1), 287-296. Retrieved from http://www.abanet.org

[126] Nayelof, J. L., Fuchs, S. C., & Moreira, L. B. (2012). Meta-analyses and forest plots using a Microsoft Excel spreadsheet: Step-by-step guide focusing on descriptive data analysis. *BMC Research Notes, 5*, 52-57. doi:10.1186/1756-0500-5-52

[127] Newell, E. (2008). Turn yourselves in. *Government Executive, 40*(4), 28-33. Retrieved from www.govexec.com

[128] Newman, I., Lim, J., & Pineda, F. (2013). Content validity using a mixed method approach: Its application and development through the use of a table of specifications methodology. *Journal of Mixed Methods Research, 7*, 243-260. doi:10.1177/1558689813476922

[129] Ni, N., Qian, C., & Crilly, D. (2014). The stakeholder enterprise: Caring for community be attending to employees. *Strategic Organization, 12*, 38-61. doi:10.1177/1476127013510239

[130] Nind, M., Wiles, R., Bengry-Howell, A., & Crow, G. (2013). Methodological innovation and research ethics: Forces in tension or forces in harmony? *Qualitative Research, 13*, 650-667. doi:10.1177/1468794112455042

[131] Noordegraaf, M. (2011). Risky business: How professional fields (must) deal with organizational issues. *Organization Studies, 32*, 1349-1371. doi:10.1177/0170840611416748

[132] O'Kelly, C., & Wheeler, S. (2012). Internalities and the foundations of corporate governance. *Social & Legal Studies, 21*, 469-489. doi:10.1177/0964663912453374

[133] O'Reilly, K., Paper, D., & Marx, S. (2012). Demystifying grounded theory for business research. *Organizational Research Methods, 15*, 247-262. doi:10.1177/1094428111434559

[134] Office of the Inspector General: United States Department of Justice (USDOJ). (2010). *Investigations press releases*. Retrieved from http://www.justice.gov/oig/press/inv-press.htm

[135] Offstein, E. H., Dufresne, R. L., & Childers, J. S. (2012). Reconciling competing tensions in ethical systems: Lessons from the United States Military Academy at West Point. *Group & Organization Management, 37*, 617-654. doi:10.1177/1059601112456594

[136] Ohemeng, F. L. K., & Grant, J. K. (2014). Neither public nor private: The efficacy of mixed model public service delivery in two Canadian municipalities. *Canadian Public administration, 57*, 548-572. doi:10.1111/capa.12090

[137] Orndoff, C., & Papkov, G. (2012). Effect of the 2009 American Recovery and Reinvestment Act (ARRA) on civil engineering. *Journal of Professional Issues in Engineering Education & Practice, 138*, 2-9. doi:10.1061/(ASCE)EI.1943-5541.0000073

[138] Parboteeah, K., Chen, H., Lin, Y., Chen, I., Lee, A. P., & Chung, A. (2010). Establishing organizational ethical climates: How do managerial practices work?. *Journal of Business Ethics, 97*(4), 599-611. doi:10.1007/s10551-010-0527-9

[139] Payton, S. B., & Kennedy, S. S. (2013). Fiscal magic: Outsourcing and the taxing power. *State and Local Government Review, 45*, 189-195. doi:10.1177/0160323X13494859

[140] Perry, D. J. (2013). Transcendental method for research with human subjects: A transformative phenomenology for the human sciences. *Field Methods, 25*, 262-282. doi:10.1177/1525822X12467105

[141] Pezalla, A., Pettigrew, J., Miller-Day, M. (2012). Researching the researcher-as-instrument: An exercise in interviewer self-reflexivity. *Qualitative Research, 12*(2), 165-185. doi:10.1177/1468794111422107

[142] Pimentel, J. C., Kuntz, J. R., & Elenkov, D. S. (2010). Ethical decision-making: an integrative model for business practice. *European Business Review, 22*(4), 359.

[143] Ram, M., Woldesenbet, K., & Jones, T. (2011). Raising the 'table stakes'? Ethnic minority businesses and supply chain relationships. *Society, 25*, 309-326. doi:10.1177/0950017011398896

[144] Renouard, C. (2011). Corporate social responsibility, utilitarianism, and the capabilities approach. *Journal of Business Ethics, 98*, 85-97. doi:10.1007/s10551-010-0536-8

[145] Resnik, B. B. (2011). Scientific research and the public trust. *Science and Engineering Ethics, 17*, 399-409. doi:10.1007/s11948-010-9210-x

[146] Reybold, L. E., Lammert, J. D., & Stribling, S. M. (2013). Participant selection as a conscious research method: Thinking forward and the deliberation of 'emergent' findings. *Qualitative Research, 13*, 699-716. doi:10.1177/1468794112465634

[147] Rhodes, C., & Wray-Bliss, E. (2013). The ethical difference of organization. *Organization, 20*, 39-50. doi:10.1177/1350508412460999

[148] Richman, V., & Richman, A. (2011). A tale of two perspectives: Regulation versus self-regulation. A financial reporting approach (from Sarbanes-Oxley) for research ethics. *Science & Engineering Ethics, 18*, 241-246. doi:10.1007/s11948-011-9260-8

[149] Robbins, D., Shaw, S. A., Grandon, R. A., Sears, B., & Eldridge, A. (2011). Path of an investigation: How a major contractor's ethics office and air force procurement fraud and suspension/debarment apparatus deal with allegations of potential fraud and unethical conduct. *Public Contract Law Journal, 40*, 595-617. Retrieved from http://pclj.org/

[150] Roberts, R. N. (2010). Mandatory contractor codes of ethics and defense procurement integrity. *Journal of Public Procurement, 2*(2), 247-274. Retrieved from http://pracademics.com

[151] Robinson, S. G. (2013). The relevancy of ethnography to nursing research. *Nursing Science Quarterly, 26*, 14-19. doi:10.1177/0894318412466742

[152] Rosenbloom, D. H. (2013). Reflections on "public administrative theory and the separation of powers". *American Review of Public Administration, 43*, 381-396. doi:10.1177/0275074013483167

[152a] Rotter, J. P., Airlike, P., & Mark-Herbert, C. (2014). Exloring political corporate social responsibility in global supply chain management. *Journal of Business Ethics, 125*, 581-599. doi:10.1007/s10551-013-1927-4

[153] Rousseau, J. (1984). *A discourse on inequality.* (M. Cranston, Trans.). New York, NY: Penguin Books. (Original work published 1910)

[154] Rowe, J., & Kellam, C. (2011). Ethics and moral development: Core ingredients of a compliance culture. *Home Health Care Management & Practice, 23*, 55-59. doi:10.1177/1084822310382020

[155] Rufin, C., & Rivera-Santos, M. (2012). Between commonweal and competition: Understanding the governance of public-private partnerships. *Journal of Management, 38*, 1634-1654. doi:10.1177/0149206310373948

[156] Scherer, A. G., Baumann-Pauly, D., & Schneider, A. (2013). Democratizing corporate governance: Compensating for the democratic deficit of corporate political activity and corporate citizenship. *Business & Society, 52*, 473-514. doi:10.1177/0007650312446931

[157] Schick, R. (2011). Government contracting: From the perspectives of management, ethics, and governance. *Public Administration Review, 71*, 665-667. doi:10.1111/j.1540-6210.2011.02403

[158] Schoorman, D., & Bogotch, I. (2010). What is a critical multicultural researcher? A self-reflective study of the role of the researcher. *Education, Citizenship, and Social Justice, 5*, 249-264. doi:10.1177/1746197910382257

[159] Schumacher, E. G., & Wasieleski, D. M. (2013). Institutionalizing ethical innovations in organizations: An integrated casual model of moral innovation decision process. *Journal of Business Ethics, 113*, 15-37. doi:10.1007/s10551-012-1277-7

[160] Sebastian, R. J., & Davison, B. (2011). The root causes of contract administration problems. *Journal of Public Procurement, 11*(2), 171-189. Retrieved from http://pracademics.com

[161] Segal, L. (2012). Instilling stewardship to address the integrity/efficiency dilemma. *Administration & Society, 44*, 825-852. doi:10.1177/0095399711427533

[162] Servon, L. J., Fairlie, R. W., Rastello, B., & Seely, A. (2010). The five gaps facing small and microbusiness owners: Evidence from New York City. *Economic Development Quarterly, 24*, 126-142. doi:10.1177/0891242409354899

[163] Shadnam, M. (2014). Heterologous and homologous perspectives on the relation between morality and organization: Illustration of implications for studying the rise of private military and security industry. *Journal of Management Inquiry, 23*, 22-37. doi:10.1177/1056492612472555

[164] Sharp, J. L., Mobley, C., Hammond, C., Withington, C., Drew, S., Stringfield, S., & Stipanovic, N. (2011). A mixed methods sampling methodology for a multisite case study. *Journal of Mixed Methods Research, 6*, 34-54. doi:10.1177/1558689811417133

[165] Sheehan, N., & Stabell, C. (2010). Reputation as a driver in activity level analysis: Reputation and competitive advantage in knowledge intensive firms. *Corporate Reputation Review, 13*, 198-208. doi:10.1057/crr.2010.19

[166] Singh, J. B. (2011). Determinants of the effectiveness of corporate codes of ethics: An empirical study. *Journal of Business Ethics, 101*, 385-395. doi:10.1007/s10551-010-0727-3

[167] Sinocruz, J. Q., Hildebrand, E. A., Neuman, B. L., & Branaghan, R. J. (2011). Human factors implications for standard operating procedure development and usability in reprocessing safety. *Human Factors and Ergonomics Society Annual Meeting. Proceedings, 55*, 803-807. doi:10.1177/1071181311551166

[168] Smallbone, D., Kitching, J., & Athayde, R. (2010). Ethnic diversity, entrepreneurship and competitiveness in a global city. *International Small Business Journal, 28*, 174-190. doi:10.1177/0266242609355856

169 Smirnova, O. V., & Leland, S. M. (2014). The role of power and competition in contracting out: An analysis of public transportation markets. *Administration & Society, 46*, 1-23. doi:10.1177/0095399713498748

170 Smith, C. R., & Fernandez, S. (2010). Equity in federal contracting: Examining the link between minority representation and federal procurement decisions. *Public Administration Review, 70*, 87-96. doi:10.1111/j.1540-6210.2009.02113x

171 Sonpar, K. (2011). Stakeholder theory: The state of the art. *M@n@gement, 14*, 210-220. doi:10.3917/mana.143.0210

172 Stanger, A. (2012). Transparency as a core public value and mechanism of compliance. *Criminal Justice Ethics, 31*(3), 287-301. Retrieved from http://www.tandf.co.uk/journals/titles/0731129X.asp

173 Stewart, J. (2012). Multiple-case study methods in governance-related research. *Public Management Review, 14*, 67-82. doi:10. 1080/14719037.2011.589618

174 Suarez-Ortega, M. (2013). Performance, reflexivity, and learning through biographical-narrative research. *Qualitative Inquiry, 19*, 189-200. doi:10.1177/1077800412466223

175 Suri, H. (2011). Purposeful sampling in qualitative research synthesis. *Qualitative Research Journal (RMIT Training Pty Ltd Trading As RMIT Publishing), 11*, 63-75. doi:10.3316/QRJ1102063

176 Sussman, S. (2011). Introduction to Issue on Qualitative Research and Evidence-Based Practices. *Evaluation & The Health Professions, 34*, 255-257. doi:10.1177/0163278711418901

177 Svara, J. H. (2014). Who Are the Keepers of the Code? Articulating and Upholding Ethical Standards in the Field of Public Administration. *Public Administration Review, 74*, 561-569. doi:10.1111/puar.12230

178 Tomescu, M., & Popescu, M. A. (2013). Ethics and conflicts of interest in the public sector. *Contemporary Readings in Law and Social Justice, 5*(2), 201-206. Retrieved from www.contemporaryscienceassociation.net

179 Tota, I., & Shehu, H. (2012). The dilemma of business ethics. *Journal of Emerging Market Finance, 3*, 555-559. doi:10.1016/S2212-5671(12)00195-5

180 Tozzo, B. (2013). Can theories of empire explain the American political response to the financial crisis? *Critical Sociology, 39*, 9-20. doi:10.1177/0896920511415298

181 Tracy, S. J. (2013). *Qualitative research methods: Collecting evidence, crafting analysis, communicating impact.* Malden, MA: Wiley-Blackwell. Tracy, S. J. (2013). *Qualitative research methods: Collecting evidence, crafting analysis, communicating impact.* Malden, MA: Wiley-Blackwell.

[182]   Turner, P. K., & Norwood, K. M. (2013). Body of research: Impetus, instrument, and impediment. *Qualitative Inquiry, 19,* 696-711. doi:10.1177/1077800413500928

[183]   Van den Steen, E. (2010). On the origin of shared beliefs (and corporate culture). *RAND Journal of Economics (Blackwell Publishing Limited), 41*(4), 617-648. doi:10.1111/j.1756-2171.2010.00114.x

[184]   Van Milligen, M. C. (2012). Organized outsourcing commentary. *Public Administration Review, 72,* 817-818. doi:10.111/j.1540-6210.2012.02638.x

[185]   Vandenberg, H., & Hall, W. (2011). Critical ethnography: Extending attention to bias and reinforcement of dominant power relations. *Nurse Researcher, 18*(3), 25-30. Retrieved from http://nurseresearcher.rcnpublishing.co.uk

[186]   VanderWalde, A., & Kurzban, S. (2011). Paying human subjects in research: Where are we, how did we get here, and now what? *Journal of Law, Medicine, & Ethics, 39,* 543-558. doi:10.1111/j.1748-720X.2011.00621

[187]   Verhulst, S. (2010). The regulation of digital content. In L. Lievrouw, & S. Livingstone (Eds.), *Handbook of new media: Social shaping and social consequences of ICTs, updated student edition* (pp. 329-350). doi:10.4135/9781446211304.n18

[188]   Waite, D. (2014). Teaching the unteachable: Some issues of qualitative research pedagogy. *Qualitative Inquiry, 20,* 267-281. doi:10.1177/1077800413489532

[189]   Walker, J. L. (2012). Research column. The use of saturation in qualitative research. *Canadian Journal of Cardiovascular Nursing, 22*(2), 37-46. Retrieved from http://www.cccn.ca

[190]   Wallace, T. L. (2011). An argument-based approach to validity in evaluation. *Evaluation, 17,* 233-246. doi:10.1177/1356389011410522

[191]   Warren, D. E., Gasper, J. P., & Laufer, W. S. (2014). Is formal ethics training merely cosmetics? A study of ethics training and ethical organizational culture. *Business Ethics Quarterly, 24,* 85-117. doi: 10.5840/beq2014233

[192]   Watkins, D. C. (2012). Qualitative research: The importance of conducting research that doesn't count. *Health Promotion Practice, 13,* 153-158. doi:10.1177/1524839912437370

[193]   Witesman, E. M., & Fernandez, S. (2013). Government contracts with private organizations: Are there differences between nonprofits and for-profits? *Nonprofit and Voluntary Sector Quarterly, 42,* 689-715. doi:10.1177/0899764012442592

[194]   Witko, C. (2011). Campaign contributions, access, and government contracting. *Journal of Public Administration Research and Theory, 21,* 761-778. doi:10.1093/jopart/mur005

[195] Yang, K. (2012). Further understanding accountability in public organizations: Actionable knowledge and the structure – agency duality. *Administration & Society, 44*, 255-284. doi:10.1177/0095399711417699

[196] Yang, K., & VanLandingham, G. (2012). How hollow can we go? A case study of the Florida's efforts to outsource oversight of privatized child welfare services. *American Review of Public Administration, 42*, 543-561. doi:10.1177/0275074011411910

[197] Yilmaz, K. (2013). Comparison of quantitative and qualitative research traditions: Epistemological, theoretical, and methodological differences. *European Journal of Education, 48*(2), 311-325. Retrieved from http://www.wiley.com

[198] Yin, R. K. (2011). *Qualitative research from start to finish*. New York, NY: The Guilford Press.

[199] Yin, R. K. (2013). Validity and generalization in future case study evaluations. *Evaluation, 19*, 321-332. doi:10.1177/1356389013497081

[200] Zachariadis, M., Scott, S., & Barrett, M. (2013). Methodological implications of critical realism for mixed-methods research. *MIS Quarterly, 37*(3), 855-879. Retrieved from http://www.misq.org/index/html

[201] Zaidi, S., Mayhew, S. H., Cleland, J., & Green, A. T. (2012). Context matters in NGO-government contracting for health service delivery: A case study from Pakistan. *Health Policy & Planning, 27*(7), 570-581. Retrieved from heapol.oxfordjournals.org

[202] Zhang, J., Chiu, R., & Wei, L. (2009). Decision-Making Process of Internal Whistleblowing Behavior in China: Empirical Evidence and Implications. *Journal of Business Ethics*, 8825-8841. doi:10.1007/s10551-008-9831-z

[203] Zhong, C. (2011). The ethical dangers of deliberative decision making. *Administrative Science Quarterly, 56*, 1-25. doi:10.2189/asqu.2011.56.1.001

www.ingramcontent.com/pod-product-compliance
Lightning Source LLC
Chambersburg PA
CBHW020535290526
45786CB00002B/894